Monica,
Leaders lead regardless of environment. May God bless you and your family.
Vinnie

TRUE LEADERSHIP:

LEADERSHIP LESSONS INSPIRED BY THE APOSTLE PAUL

PAUL "VINNIE" VENTURELLA

TRUE LEADERSHIP

*Leadership Lessons
Inspired by the Apostle Paul*

Vinnie Venturella

TRUE LEADERSHIP:

Leadership Lessons Inspired by the Apostle Paul

published by Master Press

© 2012 by Paul "Vinnie" Venturella
All rights reserved
Cover design by Kim Taylor (kimiweb.com)

Scripture taken from the
HOLY BIBLE, NEW INTERNATIONAL VERSION®
Copyright © 1973, 1978, 1984 by International Bible Society.
Used by permission of Zondervan.
All rights reserved

Printed in the United States

ALL RIGHTS RESERVED
No part of this publication may be reproduced, stored in a retrieval system, or transmitted, in any form or by any means—electronic, mechanical, photocopying, recording, or otherwise—without written permission

True Leadership:
Leadership Lessons Inspired by the Apostle Paul
ISBNL 978-0-9790296-9-1

For information:

MASTER PRESS
3405 ISLAND BAY WAY, KNOXVILLE, TN 37931
Mail to: publishing@ masterpressbooks.com

*This book is dedicated to my two daughters
Meaghan and Sophia.
They are beautiful in mind, body and spirit.
My prayer is they will live life to the fullest,
doing God's will.*

ACKNOWLEDGEMENTS

This book could not have been completed without the help of many. I felt led to write it. Interestingly, all those who assisted me are terrific leaders in their respective environments. Where would this world be without leaders?

Rex Freriks and Michael Lamonica are my two best friends, and my most prolific supporters and encouragers. They were a constant voice of motivation. They offered the very first edits and course corrections of my book. Both have been leaders for two-plus decades and offered me insight no one else could. Rex's Mom Connie also offered her editing expertise, inspiration and encouragement. Christian moms have such awesome responsibility and play such a phenomenal role as an example for their kids.

Ken Rodriguez (USAF Colonel Retired) and Steven Schaick (USAF Chaplain Colonel; endorsed by the Presbyterian Church (USA)) have been mentors of mine. I met Ken in the early nineties and Steve in 2005. Both are very knowledgeable of the Bible and terrific leaders. They provided the strong hand that I needed in their editing.

I am grateful to have Chad Montgomery (USAF Chaplain Captain) in my life. He is a maturing leader and his humility is unmatched. He was a constant steady voice of reason and encouragement. We all need Chad Montgomery's in our life.

Dr. Ron Crews BA, MDiv, DMin (USAR Colonel Retired; Endorsing Agent Grace Churches International) has been a mentor since I met him in early 2010. I was drawn to Manna Church one day and as fate would have it Ron was in his office when a young man Kyle introduced us. I told Ron about my book, and he immediately encouraged me to take his class on Romans (which I did). He prayed for me then, and has prayed for me ever since. He gave me the most pointed feedback on my format and content. Leaders lead, and sometimes when we need tough love, leaders need to give it. Ron is a great man, a great leader, and a great friend.

Ron led me to Michael Cotton, who led me to Neil Silverberg from MasterPressBooks. Neil, thank God, led me to Sheila Atchley. Sheila has forgotten more about writing and using the English language than I'll ever know. She batted clean-up, and provided the final editing of this book. We've never met in person, and I hope to fix that soon. But over the phone and email, we've built a good relationship. I cannot thank Sheila enough for what she has done for me and this project.

CONTENTS

Acknowledgements..vii

PART 1

Introduction.. 3
Leadership As I See It..................................... 7
Are Leaders Born Or Made 9
Paul's Mission... 11

PART 2

LEADERSHIP LESSONS INSPIRED BY THE APOSTLE PAUL

True Teammates Have Your Back........................... 17
Standing Up For A New Leader 19
Standing Up Against The Bad Guy........................ 21
Always Ready.. 22

Focus On Your Mission 23
When In The Face of Opposition 24
Don't Let Popularity Go To Your Head 25
Some Leaders Are Tough 26
Offer Encouragement. 27
Appoint Leaders. 28
After Action Reports 29
Trusted Leaders Handle Urgent And Important Matters 31
Management By Walking Around 33
Make The Tough Call. 35
Consistent Leaders Throughout An Organization. 36
Always Maintain Your Demeanor. 37
Using Facts To Persuade 39
The Master Communicator 41
Know When To Say When. 43
Leaders Also Need Reassurance 45
Leaders Are Trainers 47
Leaders May Be Falsely Attacked 49
Leaders Continue Their Work Despite The Time 51
Selfless Sacrifice 53
Constantly Mentor Upcoming Leaders. 55
Lead By Example 57
A Higher Calling 59
True Leaders Don't Seek Man's Favor 61
How Far Are You Willing To Go 63
Staying On Message. 64
All The Way. 65
The Power Of Public Speech. 67
Be Bold 69

Restatement Of Mission	70
Rewarded For What You Do	71
What To Do	73
What Not To Do	74
Character Revealed	75
Predestined	77
Leaders Grow	79
Use Your Gifts	80
Honor One Another	81
Do The Right Thing	82
Live At Peace With Everyone	83
The Bottom Line	85
Be Direct	87
Be On Guard	89
Establishing Authority	91
Perfectly United	92
Build On The Foundation	93
Faithful Service	95
Leaders Are Always On Display	96
Provide Ready Leaders	97
Imitate Me	99
Do Not Air Your Dirty Laundry	100
Get Rid Of The Bad Apple	101
When In Rome Do As The Romans Do...With One Exception	103
Strive For The True Prize	105
Unity Of The Team	107
Use Your Gifts For The Common Good	109
Synergy	110
Diversity	111

All Are Important 112

All For One And One For All 113

Leaders Are Organized 114

Humble In Your Position 115

Don't Be Misled By Bad Doctrine 116

Your Work Is Not In Vain 117

Be Strong In Your Faith 118

Leaders Have Compassion 119

Rumor Control 120

Do Not Lose Heart 121

To Live On 122

Do Not Be Yoked Together With Unbelievers 123

Tough Love 125

Be A Cheerful Giver 126

Be A Sower 127

Boast In The Lord 129

Always Be Authentic 130

What You Need To Be A Good Public Speaker 131

Keep On Doing What I'm Doing 133

Suffering For Mission Completion 134

Showing Genuine Concern For Your People 135

God Given Authority Is Meant To Build Up 136

A Leader Amongst Leaders 137

Saying No When All Around You Are Saying Yes 139

The Common Denominators 140

BLUF 141

What Is Your Mission? 142

The Foundation Of An Organization 143

Commander's Intent 144

Live A Worthy Life	145
Some Are Destined To Be Leaders	147
The Whole Body	148
Lead By Building Up	149
Strive To Live Wisely; With Wisdom	150
Training And Instruction	151
Good Work Will Get Rewarded	152
Equip Your Team	153
Declare It Fearlessly	154
Lead From The Front	155
Leaders Are Humble	157
Praise In Public	158
Some Things Just Don't Matter	159
Change When You Know You Must	160
Correction Does Not Mean Conflict	161
Put What I've Taught You Into Practice	162
Sharing The Good News	163
A Leader's Impact	164
Don'ts	165
Encourage Your Children	167
Working With All Your Heart	168
Bragging About Your People To Others	169
Vector Check	170
Thank Your People	171
Be A Model To Emulate	172
Constantly Nurture	173
Shared Pain Brings People Closer Together	174
Being An Example	175
Build Each Other Up	176

Know Your Role. 177
Acknowledge Perseverance 178
Reiterate Sound Doctrine. 179
Exceeding The Standard. 180
Peer Pressure Works 181
Never Tire Of Doing What Is Right. 183
A Pure Heart 184
He Is In Charge 185
Where Have You Been 186
Qualities Of Leaders. 187
Leaders Must Be Above Reproach. 189
Leadership Is A Noble Task 191
Reputation Is What Others Say About You. 192
Leaders Must Be Tested 193
Overcome Youth With Example. 195
Faith, Family And Everything Else 197
Guard What Has Been Entrusted. 199
A Good Soldier 200
Leaders Must Develop Others Leaders 201
Pleasing The Leader 203
Steer Clear Of Fools And Stupidity 204
Leaders Are Always Prepared 205
Going All The Way. 206
Stand Strong Even If By Yourself 207
Encourage And Rebuke With Authority. 208
Leaders Delegate 209
Do The Basics Extraordinarily Well 211
Be An Example For Young People 213
Instructions With Divisive People 215

Appeal In A Way Aside From Rank 216
We're All Useful For Someone 217
The Silver Lining 219
Appealing To A Man's Heart And Character. 220

PART 3

Conclusion. 223
Selected Scripture. 225

PART 1

INTRODUCTION

In June 2007, I invited Shawn Withy-Allen to address the opening of our Vacation Bible School of my former church. Shawn and I met in the business community, and we are now friends. Currently, he is the director of RUSH Campus ministries, and the Student Ministries pastor for Manna Church, the church where my family and I belong. Shawn also baptized my daughter Meaghan in July 2011.

Shawn opened our VBS with a prayer and commented "I'd like to talk to you about one of my heroes…Paul." Then he read some Scripture from one of Paul's letters. I recollect some general thoughts about Paul and the Bible. But Shawn's presence, his demeanor, and his message stuck with me. I, too, had thought a lot about Paul.

Convinced I had so much more to learn about life, leadership, and my God, in July 2007 I committed to reading the Bible every day. I made it my goal to read the whole Bible cover to cover before the end of 2007. I was pretty familiar with most of the popular stories, but once I started making Bible reading a daily commitment, it enriched my life in amazing ways. My reading also led me to a new fascination with Paul, and built an insatiable appetite to learn more about him.

During one of my readings around April 2008, I felt "something" influencing me to write a book about the Apostle Paul, so I did. I am a student of leadership. I read about leadership, I study it, I write about it, I teach it, and I execute its principles. My first book *Character, Competence, and Commitment…the Measure of a Leader* (Authorhouse.com) was a reflection of my 21+ year career in a unique and elite USAF Special Operations environment.

This book's theme is *True Leadership* as defined and demonstrated by the Apostle Paul. After Jesus, Paul was the most influential leader in Christianity. That took faith, hope, and love. It also took perseverance and whole lot of passion. Leadership principles pervade almost every single situation in Paul's life and ministry. The same could be said of us, for there are endless opportunities to lead and be led in a lifetime.

When you read and study Acts and all of Paul's letters, you can't help but be amazed at what this man did. I marvel at what he went through (beaten, lost at sea, walked thousands of miles, stoned, flogged, imprisoned, and executed). I am intrigued at the sheer magnitude of his mission. I am thankful for the immense influence this man had on the largest religion in the world. I realize there are leadership lessons for every believer throughout Paul's writings.

This book is a byproduct of my own ministry. I first want to glorify God. I attempt to do this by exposing readers to His Word. I believe God will be glorified, if the reader gleans at least some of the leadership nuggets through God's Word as they pertain to Paul.

Just because I wrote this book does not, by any means, imply that I am perfect in the area of leadership application. I fail to live up to these ideals every day. Failure doesn't mean I am not saved. It does not mean that I can't teach these principles. I strive every day to glorify Him. I am thankful for His grace and know I am under construction each and every day.

My personal mission is to positively influence lives. I do this through various avenues, and most specifically through Faith, Family and Finance. I try my best to be a positive influence regardless of environment. It is my prayer that God will use these words to impart knowledge to the reader, and inspire some form of action by the reader. I will not attempt to make a Biblical translation or hermeneutical assessment of Paul's words; instead I will articulate simple, but profound leadership lessons that have influenced me, taken from the verses I will cite for you.

We gain so much in our own walk by consistently and persistently studying God's inspired Word. These verses can teach us so much, if we let them. So let's get started on some leadership lessons through Paul's writings and experiences, as laid out in the Bible.

SOME ASSUMPTIONS

Throughout this book, I use the information found in Scripture. I acknowledge if something is my opinion or implied.

All Bible references are from the *New International Version.*

I write in the male vernacular. I don't use *"he or she," "him or her."*

I write like I speak.

I reference the *Old Testament* and *New Testament* as appropriate. They weren't called that back in Paul's day.

LEADERSHIP AS I SEE IT

Leadership is influence. Leadership is making things happen. Leadership is about influencing people toward accomplishing an objective or task. Good leadership means the followers "want" to do what the leader wants them to do. Leadership is inspiring people to do more than they think they can. True leadership encapsulates all that is good about leadership. True leadership glorifies God, edifies others, and builds His Kingdom.

Thousands of books have been written about leadership. The reason there are thousands of books on leadership is because there are thousands of opinions on how or why to influence, to inspire, to make things happen, or to get people to accomplish some task. You have to influence people to get things done. How a leader influences people will vary from leader to leader, and some do it better than others.

In summary, my mission is to *Positively Influence Lives*.

Positively: In a manner that is focused on Him, inspiring, empathetic, nurturing, team focused, respectful, trustworthily, with character, with competence, with commitment, loyally, and with accountability.

Influence: Leadership (across the spectrum).

Lives: Anyone, everyone, regardless of age, gender, status, or environment.

I believe leadership pervades every aspect of life. Our homes, churches, military, our athletics, business, for profit, not-for-profit, government spheres, and social structures - all have leaders and leadership opportunities. Obviously, some environments are more leadership-focused than others, but all environments, if they involve more than one person have to utilize leaders. The question is, are the leaders good or bad, effective or ineffective?

I have tried to be a good leader in every aspect of my life. I have many failures and I have many successes. I never stop trying to be better in all areas of my life, and leadership is one of the most important areas to focus on becoming better.

ARE LEADERS BORN OR MADE

There has always been a great debate about whether leaders are born or made. Conventional wisdom, (and most people I've heard speak or write on the subject of leadership) state that leaders are made. In my maturation (as a Christian, leader, and man) I have some compelling thoughts that leaders are *also* born. Ultimately, I believe both. Leaders are born *and* made. I lean toward made for obvious reasons, but I also choose to disagree with anyone who says leaders cannot be born.

Jeremiah 1:4-5 states *The word of the Lord came to me, saying, "Before I formed you in the womb I knew you, before you were born I set you apart; I appointed you as a prophet to the nations."* Jeremiah states how God "predestined" him to be a prophet.

Paul also says in Galatians 1:15 *"But when God, who set me apart from birth and called me by his grace,…"* acknowledges here in this passage that God's plan started at the very beginning.

And of course in Psalm 139:13 *For you created my inmost being; you knit me together in my mother's womb.* This again signifies that God has a plan for His children and that plan is started before birth.

Most Christians I've met believe in fate, and most Christians I've met believe the life we are living is predestined, meaning: it is all part of God's plan, albeit a plan in which God gives us the ability to make our own choices. If that is the case, then God plans for certain people to be leaders, just as he plans for certain people to be elected officials, entertainers, missionaries, soldiers, ministers, etc.

I believe God has a plan for all of us. And I believe that God puts tools in our toolboxes to enable that plan. If it is leadership He wants you to undertake, then He enables you through tools, education, experiences, opportunities, and challenges to become a leader to do His will.

I believe that, over time additional tools are put in your toolbox, and you become a better leader through experience, study, trial and error, mentorship, practice, tribulations, desire, etc. Some leaders don't come to fruition, and others have a knack for it and naturally become leaders, but I believe that since God has a plan for all of us, He puts the tools there that we will need to conduct that plan, either at birth and/or along the way.

PAUL'S MISSION

All leaders have a mission. All leaders have some form of objectives or goals which they are attempting to achieve with other people. Without a mission and people to carry out the mission, we would not need leaders. Paul's mission was God-ordained. Paul was the Apostle to the Gentiles. Paul's mission was preaching/teaching the Good News (gospel) to the Gentiles (Acts 9:16; Acts 22:21; Acts 26:16-18)

Here are some verses that remind us of Paul's mission:

But the Lord said to Ananias, "Go! This man is my chosen instrument to carry my name before the Gentiles and their kings and before the people of Israel. I will show him how much he must suffer for my name." (Acts 9:15-16) *While they were worshiping the Lord and fasting, the Holy Spirit said, "Set apart for me Barnabas and Saul for the work to which I have called them."* (Acts 13:2) *From Attalia they sailed back to Antioch, where they had been committed to the grace of God for the work they had now completed.* (Acts 14:26) *One night the Lord spoke to Paul in a vision: "Do not be afraid; keep on speaking, do not be silent. For I am with you, and no one is going to attack and harm you, because I have many people in this city."* (Acts 18:9-10) *However, I consider my life worth nothing to me, if only I may finish the race and complete the task the Lord Jesus has given me—the task of testifying to the gospel of God's grace.* (Acts 20:24) *"Then he said: 'The God of our fathers has chosen you to know his will and to see the Righteous One and to hear words from his mouth. You will be his witness to all men of what you have seen and heard.* (Acts 22:14-15) *"Then the Lord said to me, 'Go; I will send you far away to the Gentiles.'"* (Acts 22:21) *The following night the Lord stood near Paul and said, "Take courage! As you have testified about me in Jerusalem, so you must also testify in Rome."* (Acts 23:11) *"Then I asked, 'Who are you, Lord?' 'I am Jesus, whom you are persecuting,' the Lord replied. 'Now get up and stand on your feet. I have appeared to you to appoint you as a servant and as a witness of what you have seen of me and what I will show you. I will rescue you from your own people and from the Gentiles. I am sending you to them to open their eyes and turn them from darkness to light, and from the power of Satan to God, so that they may receive forgiveness of sins and a place among those who are sanctified by faith in me.'* (Acts 26:15-18)

Paul, a servant of Christ Jesus, called to be an apostle and set apart for the gospel of God— (Rom 1:1) *I am talking to you Gentiles. Inasmuch as I am the apostle to the Gentiles, I make much of my ministry in the hope that I may somehow arouse my own people to envy and save some of them.* (Rom 11:13-14) *I have written you quite boldly on some points, as if to remind you of them again, because of the grace God gave me to be a minister of Christ Jesus to the Gentiles with the priestly duty of proclaiming the gospel of God, so that the Gentiles might become an offering acceptable to God, sanctified by the Holy Spirit.* (Rom 15:15-16)

Paul, called to be an apostle of Christ Jesus by the will of God, and our brother Sosthenes, (1 Cor 1:1) *Am I not free? Am I not an apostle? Have I not seen Jesus our Lord? Are you not the result of my work in the Lord? Even though I may not be an apostle to others, surely I am to you! For you are the seal of my apostleship in the Lord.* (1 Cor 9:1-2) *Paul, an apostle of Christ Jesus by the will of God, and Timothy our brother, To the church of God in*

Corinth, together with all the saints throughout Achaia: (2 Cor 1:1) *This is why I write these things when I am absent, that when I come I may not have to be harsh in my use of authority—the authority the Lord gave me for building you up, not for tearing you down.* (2 Cor 13:10)

Paul, an apostle—sent not from men nor by man, but by Jesus Christ and God the Father, who raised him from the dead— (Gal 1:1) *I want you to know, brothers, that the gospel I preached is not something that man made up. I did not receive it from any man, nor was I taught it; rather, I received it by revelation from Jesus Christ.* (Gal 1:11-12) *But when God, who set me apart from birth and called me by his grace, was pleased to reveal his Son in me so that I might preach him among the Gentiles, I did not consult any man,* (Gal 1:15-16) *On the contrary, they saw that I had been entrusted with the task of preaching the gospel to the Gentiles, just as Peter had been to the Jews. For God, who was at work in the ministry of Peter as an apostle to the Jews, was also at work in my ministry as an apostle to the Gentiles.* (Gal 2:7-8) *Paul, an apostle of Christ Jesus by the will of God, To the saints in Ephesus, the faithful in Christ Jesus:* (Eph 1:1) *For this reason I, Paul, the prisoner of Christ Jesus for the sake of you Gentiles—Surely you have heard about the administration of God's grace that was given to me for you, that is, the mystery made known to me by revelation, as I have already written briefly.* (Eph 3:1-3) *I became a servant of this gospel by the gift of God's grace given me through the working of his power. Although I am less than the least of all God's people, this grace was given me: to preach to the Gentiles the unsearchable riches of Christ,* (Eph 3:7-8) *I have become its servant by the commission God gave me to present to you the word of God in its fullness—* (Col 1:25)

On the contrary, we speak as men approved by God to be entrusted with the gospel. We are not trying to please men but God, who tests our hearts. (1 Thes 2:4) *Paul, an apostle of Christ Jesus by the command of God our Savior and of Christ Jesus our hope,* (1 Tim 1:1) *And for this purpose I was appointed a herald and an apostle—I am telling the truth, I am not lying—and a teacher of the true faith to the Gentiles.* (1 Tim 2:7) *And of this gospel I was appointed a herald and an apostle and a teacher.* (2 Tim 1:11) *and at his appointed season he brought his word to light through the preaching entrusted to me by the command of God our Savior,* (Tit 1:3)

There is no doubt of what Paul's mission was: preaching/teaching the Good News (gospel) to the Gentiles. True leaders know their mission and drive through to completion.

PART 2

LEADERSHIP LESSONS INSPIRED BY THE APOSTLE PAUL

TRUE TEAMMATES HAVE YOUR BACK

After many days had gone by, the Jews conspired to kill him, but Saul learned of their plan. Day and night they kept close watch on the city gates in order to kill him. But his followers took him by night and lowered him in a basket through an opening in the wall.

Acts 9:23-25

Imagine if you were a Jew in Damascus and you knew who the "old" Paul was (a great persecutor of the Church) and now he's in your town as a proponent of Jesus. That's what happened following Paul's conversion. He grew more powerful (Acts 9:22) in his testimony about Jesus. Even though Paul was now a proponent of Jesus, others did not believe him.

True teammates will cover your back. Here, Paul was recently a persecutor of Christians (even though they weren't yet called that at the time) and they still protected him. Imagine a walled city with a few gates that are constantly guarded. It would be nearly impossible to pass through them undetected without some form of clandestine operation. What did Paul's brothers do? They lowered him over the wall at night in a basket.

I can't count how many times my friends, peers, or teammates covered my back. Whether it was physically, emotionally, practically or various other ways - they had my back. How does this happen? It happens through mutual trust, respect, loyalty, and a common bond – all of these are identifiable traits.

If you're in an unfriendly environment, such as war or similar dangerous surroundings, or around people of ill repute, true teammates will cover your back. In a leadership situation this protection occurs not because they have to, but because they want to. They will want to if you've inspired them, remained loyal to them, shown yourself to be trustworthy, or downright proven yourself to them.

STANDING UP FOR A NEW LEADER

But Barnabas took him and brought him to the apostles. He told them how Saul on his journey had seen the Lord and that the Lord had spoken to him, and how in Damascus he had preached fearlessly in the name of Jesus.

Acts 9:27

After Paul's conversion, he was still viewed with fear by the disciples. He had not yet proven himself. But God had other plans for Paul and it didn't matter that others didn't believe in him yet; God did. Paul learned early on in his ministry that God's opinion of him mattered far more than what others thought. Leadership begins by listening, not to the confidence or cowardice; but to God.

When you're in a new situation, oftentimes you would hope your good reputation precedes you. Whether it's good or bad, it does precede you in some manner. However, Paul's reputation wasn't good in others' opinion. What to do? When you have other respected leaders to vouch for you, that's a great start. You still have to prove yourself, but the initial vouching by Barnabas enabled Paul to start his ministry.

When another respected, seasoned leader says, "I know this guy, and he's good to go," that is usually all you need in most situations. If the seasoned leader is respected and trusted, oftentimes that's all you need. "He's one of us," is a famed line that has the same impact.

In the military, the top leader is called the commander. And commanders switch out about every two years on average. If he isn't very well known amongst the unit, then an experienced, trusted leader can vouch for him and enable some initial respect. Remember, the guy still has to earn his own way, but the initial vouching can be a major help.

STANDING UP AGAINST THE BAD GUY

Now the hand of the Lord is against you. You are going to be blind, and for a time you will be unable to see the light of the sun. Immediately mist and darkness came over him, and he groped about, seeking someone to lead him by the hand. When the proconsul saw what had happened, he believed, for he was amazed at the teaching of the Lord.

Acts 13:11-12

Paul and Barnabas were in Cyprus on Paul's first missionary journey. The proconsul was about to be converted, and Elymas the sorcerer was trying to subvert Paul's ministry. So Paul had to shut him down. Now most of us don't have the ability to exorcise demons or make people blind, but we do have the ability to stand up against the bad guy.

If a man is immoral, unethical, unlawful, or just plainly an obstacle to what is right and good, a leader must fix it. If he doesn't fix the situation, it will become an impediment to the mission. Very, very few situations involve a truly evil man. At the time it may appear a man may be possessed by the devil, or he may be just a bad guy, but strong leaders stand up for what is right.

If a leader doesn't have moral and physical courage, he won't be the leader for long. Paul had this courage. Leaders should strive for consensus and harmony, but when a man doesn't get that he doesn't get it, you've got to square it away.

ALWAYS READY

Standing up, Paul motioned with his hand and said: "Men of Israel and you Gentiles who worship God, listen to me!"

Acts 13:16

Paul and Barnabas were in Pisidian Antioch and on the Sabbath were at the synagogue. During the service Paul was asked to speak. Without hesitation, Paul spoke to those present. He excellently revisited the Old Testament and used it as a backdrop to testify about the gospel.

Leaders are always ready to lead regardless of environment. Public speaking is an area in which leaders need to be comfortable. I've delivered innumerable speeches, classes, and seminars. I always tell those striving for speaking excellence that a good public speaker has two main traits: a mastery of his subject, and a honed ability to articulate his subject.

Some good public speakers are outstanding at articulating, yet they may not be masters of their subject. When such is the case, a speaker can appear to be a master of their subject because of their mastery of delivering a speech. Faking it is a 'technique.' It's not always a good one, but at times, if handled deftly, a leader can still perform his mission.

Paul was always ready to pursue his mission: deliver the gospel to the Gentiles; no matter when, no matter what. He is a perfect example for us all.

FOCUS ON YOUR MISSION

Then Paul and Barnabas answered them boldly: "We had to speak the word of God to you first. Since you reject it and do not consider yourselves worthy of eternal life, we now turn to the Gentiles. For this is what the Lord has commanded us: "'I have made you a light for the Gentiles, that you may bring salvation to the ends of the earth.'"

Acts 13:46-47

Following three successive Sabbaths, the Jews started to get jealous of Paul, and began to talk abusively against him. Paul responded boldly, with fact and truth, focusing on his mission.

It's common in tough times that weak leaders won't stand their ground, or they will allow obstacles to stand in their way of goal accomplishment. Paul was a Jew. Paul's mission was to minister to the Gentiles, and even though he was normally at a disadvantage he never stopped.

In most environments you encounter, you will not be faced with physical danger. However, you will be faced with obstacles of various types. A truly focused leader stops at nothing to accomplish his mission

WHEN IN THE FACE OF OPPOSITION

So they shook the dust from their feet in protest against them and went to Iconium.

Acts 13:51

The word of the Lord was spreading throughout the whole region. But the Jews were still persecuting Paul. In a symbol of disdain, Paul and Barnabas *shook the dust from their feet* and went to Iconium. Even though Paul had some measure of success with the Gentiles, he had next to none with the Jews. Paul agreed to disagree with those who with knowledge still chose to reject the gospel.

Paul would never succumb to peer-pressure or threats. Leaders are talked about when times are good and bad. Leaders are talked about by good people and bad people. If you know you're right, press on with your objective. In certain circumstances it's not only okay, it's admirable to let those who are in disagreement with you know where you stand.

DON'T LET POPULARITY GO TO YOUR HEAD

"Men, why are you doing this? We too are only men, human like you. We are bringing you good news, telling you to turn from these worthless things to the living God, who made heaven and earth and sea and everything in them.

Acts 14:15

While in Lystra, Paul healed a lame man. This caused the crowd to treat Paul and Barnabas as if they were gods. Paul and Barnabas were obviously concerned about this, and shouted back to the crowd confessions of their humanity.

In sports, athletes are often told "don't read your press clippings." The secular world is full of celebrities. Some appear to handle it as well as can be expected. Popularity has a way of negatively changing some people. Leaders need to caution against letting this popularity go to their heads. President Lincoln believed that if you want to test a man's character, give him power. Paul passed the power test with flying colors.

Some leaders will become popular, famous, and placed on a pedestal. In Lystra, Paul and Barnabas were thought to be gods and they instantly refuted this and gave the credit to God. Stay grounded, be humble, stay true and don't let success go to your head. Give God the glory.

SOME LEADERS ARE TOUGH

They stoned Paul and dragged him outside the city, thinking he was dead.

Acts 14:19b

Following some of Paul's preaching to those in Lystra, some Jews from Antioch and Iconium came and won the crowd over and stoned Paul.

Read that verse again: *stoned…dragged…dead.* Can you imagine the beating it must have taken for someone to think you were dead? I'd say it must have been pretty severe. Paul was physically tough. Sure he had Luke, a physician, to care for his needs on his missionary journeys (at times), but Paul was absolutely tough.

Leaders today don't often get stoned, beat up, whipped, flogged, or manhandled - but it's still a testament to a leader who can press through any and all physical challenges.

There aren't many opportunities for me to have to physically defend myself in my nice plush office. But I am privileged to have served with some of the toughest leaders on this planet. That last sentence may sound like an exaggeration; it's not. A leader's tool kit has many tools. In some environments a full tool kit includes toughness. And in some environments it's not just a 'nice to have' tool, it's a 'have to have' necessity.

OFFER ENCOURAGEMENT

> *...strengthening the disciples and encouraging them to remain true to the faith. "We must go through many hardships to enter the kingdom of God," they said.* Acts 14:22

Paul is now returning back to the same places he had recently visited. Remember, these are new immature churches and converts, and Paul knew the value of offering encouragement and strengthening them. Without consistent encouragement, an organization, small teams, and individuals may not reach their potential.

Belief in your people is powerful. When a leader shows belief in you it's also very powerful. Paul's confidence came first and foremost from the truth that God had proclaimed to Paul; namely that God's love can outpower even the most despicable sins, and that all fall short of meeting His minimum standard. Therefore, we are saved by faith, not by our works, intellect, or influence.

Feedback and encouragement sprinkled in during a person's development have an amazing impact. Encouragement keeps the person focused on his task. It says "I'm watching you and like what I see." Or "I know you're going through some rough times, but I believe in you."

You can tell the difference in an organization when a leader offers encouragement, compared with an organization with a leader that doesn't offer it; the contrast is easily identified. Motivation, initiative, and goal achievement are all byproducts of an encouraging environment. Paul knew this, and constantly encouraged in his travels and letters.

APPOINT LEADERS

Paul and Barnabas appointed elders for them in each church and, with prayer and fasting, committed them to the Lord, in whom they had put their trust.

Acts 14:23

Paul and Barnabas delegated leadership to trusted elders. In any organization, depending on the size, there are various levels of leadership. If you create followers, you build your organization one man at a time; if you create leaders you'll force-multiply your organization. The simple scope of Paul's ministry mandated leaders at key areas, cities, and churches throughout the Roman Empire.

When a leader appoints another to leadership, he must ensure the appointee is able and willing to handle the job. I am reminded of Moses and his initial reluctance to take God up on the offer to lead Israel out of bondage and into the Promised Land. It is reckless to delegate leadership to an unable or unwilling subordinate.

Why did Paul and Barnabas delegate leadership? They needed to, for one. Churches (organizations) don't get built nor are they sustained without quality leaders at every level. But I think the key is in the last word of Acts 14:23: they *trusted* them.

Appointing leaders is a huge responsibility of higher echelon leaders. To get to the point where they have to do it, requires that they know they can count on the leader being appointed. They know they can trust him. And I would say, without trust (and some other qualities discussed throughout this book) you have nothing in the leadership realm.

AFTER ACTION REPORTS

On arriving there, they gathered the church together and reported all that God had done through them and how he had opened the door of faith to the Gentiles. And they stayed there a long time with the disciples.

Acts 14:27-28

This completed Paul's first missionary journey. The church at Antioch commissioned Paul and Barnabas to carry the message of the gospel. Acts 13 and 14 cover the terrific story of this tremendous feat. Bringing the good news back to the organization that initially sent you out has many positive impacts.

First, you've signified your mission is complete. Other members of your organization will learn from your lessons whether good or bad. You will encourage others to undertake a larger role in the organization. You will motivate and build confidence in the organization.

In the military, we used to discuss most every real-world and training mission after it occurred and oftentimes write what is known as an "After Action Report." This report has many parts to it. The most basic is this: it articulates what was done, how it was done, and the final impact of what was done. The objective is to get better. But there are endless positive attributes of going through this process called the "After Action Report."

Lieutenant General George Patton said there are no new wars - they've all been fought. Reading about history will allow you to learn from others' experiences. That is what an After Action Report is. It is a history of an event. Leaders should ensure all major events are articulated and preserved for historical, training, and improvement purposes. He should also ensure that information gets passed down to the organization.

TRUSTED LEADERS HANDLE URGENT AND IMPORTANT MATTERS

This brought Paul and Barnabas into sharp dispute and debate with them. So Paul and Barnabas were appointed, along with some other believers, to go up to Jerusalem to see the apostles and elders about this question.

Acts 15:2

The "question" was do Gentiles need to be circumcised to be saved? This was a huge issue of contention in the 1st century AD. The early church appointed Paul and Barnabas (trusted leaders) to attend what was later known as the Jerusalem Council or Jerusalem Conference. Peter and James were also in attendance. The issue was agreed upon and as they say, "*The rest is history.*"

There have been numerous times in my life when major issues needed to be resolved. On equally numerous occasions, a huge task had to be resolved. A lot of those times, the task was extremely time sensitive. On such time-sensitive, huge tasks, you need your "go-to-guy(s)." There are times when a junior leader can handle it, but when an issue is of major impact or huge magnitude, you need a trusted leader that has the authority to resolve it.

There was this one point in my Air Force career, when a massive shift in training methodology needed to be addressed. Chief Master Sergeant Tim Brown led from the front, forged consensus, coordinated details, and made it happen.

Sometimes just the mere presence of certain leaders across a large organization signifies the importance of the issue. Just their sheer horse power is enough to cut through the clutter and get the job done.

There are numerous opportunities for delegated leaders to get the job done. In most of those opportunities, delegated leadership is all you need. No senior leader should have to personally oversee every situation. But when there is an organizational impacting issue that must be addressed, it normally falls on the shoulders of your trusted senior leaders.

MANAGEMENT BY WALKING AROUND

Some time later Paul said to Barnabas, "Let us go back and visit the brothers in all the towns where we preached the word of the Lord and see how they are doing."

Acts 15:36

Paul and Barnabas were in Antioch teaching and preaching. Paul wanted to go back and visit the brothers (from his first missionary journey) to encourage and strengthen them. There again is the value of consistent strengthening and encouraging of your organization.

"Management by walking around" simply means getting out of the office and figuring out what is going on, yourself. Leaders need to be out and about. You can't lead sitting in a chair pushing out emails. Your people need to see you. They want to see you. You need their valuable perspective. Not only can you get the 'ground truth' of something but you'll also have opportunity to offer encouragement.

I knew of a commander that never left the office. I do not know the reason. Thankfully he wasn't a commander I served under. I was told by a reliable leader he lacked confidence and did not have the trust of the organization. Game over, in this instance. You might as well resign, if such is your case, since you'll have zero effect in your environment.

If you wait for problems to reach you, you'll be waiting a long time and in a lot of instances they'll never get there. Get out in the field. Get out in the shop. Get out on the street. You're the leader; you can't afford all the filters below you to get the bad or even the good news.

Leaders are out and about. They will have the constant opportunity to be seen and heard. This will enable a free flow of information. And as John Maxwell says, "…catch people doing things right."

MAKE THE TOUGH CALL

...but Paul did not think it wise to take him, because he had deserted them in Pamphylia and had not continued with them in the work.

Acts 15:38

On Paul's first missionary journey Mark left him and Barnabas (Acts 13:13). The Bible doesn't tell us why, so we can only assume. Now Paul wanted to go on another missionary journey, and Barnabas wanted to take Mark. Paul did not think it wise, since Mark deserted them before. In verse 39 it says Paul and Barnabas had a sharp disagreement and split up.

Verses 38-39 are major statements. They point to numerous lessons. One is addition by division; now instead of one team of missionaries we have two. Later, you see Paul and Silas and also Barnabas and Mark were on separate journeys. Yes, there can be a disagreement between Christian believers. Leaders have to make the tough call.

We don't know the exact reason why Mark left. But obviously it bothered Paul. And it appeared Paul no longer trusted Mark. Paul settled his differences with Mark later in scripture. So Paul made the call and refused to take Mark.

"Go along to get along" was not Paul's method. In some military schools, early in my career, we would hear "cooperate and graduate." Wrong! Leaders stand up for what is right. Leaders may have to call a spade a spade if it's the right thing to do. Leaders may want to be popular, but they know they aren't in a popularity contest.

Leaders make the tough call, even to the detriment of another person, to ensure that person does not impede the organization's progress.

CONSISTENT LEADERS THROUGHOUT AN ORGANIZATION

Judas and Silas, who themselves were prophets, said much to encourage and strengthen the brothers.

Acts 15:32

Following the Jerusalem Council, leaders were dispatched to pass on the outcome of what the church leaders decided (*i.e. the all-important "After Action Report"*). In this case Judas and Silas went to the church at Antioch and gathered everyone together and delivered the letter.

There are Biblical examples where not all the apostles agreed on 100% of the issues 100% of the time. Perfect agreement does not exist. However, organizations are propelled forward when people can set aside their disagreements. More importantly, organizations have to be consistent with make or break issues, with key principals, with core values.

Here is a great example of Judas and Silas passing on the same information as Paul and Barnabas. The message is consistent regardless of who was delivering it. You cannot afford to have members of your organization assuming the road ahead or the message will be different based on the leader delivering it.

Strong organizations have consistent leaders at every level.

ALWAYS MAINTAIN YOUR DEMEANOR

About midnight Paul and Silas were praying and singing hymns to God, and the other prisoners were listening to them.

Acts 16:25

The story of Paul, Silas, Timothy, and Luke in Philippi is great. Lydia is converted. Paul exorcises a demon from a slave girl. Then the owners who received income from the slave girl's fortune-telling falsely accused Paul and Silas, and after Paul and Silas were severely beaten, they were thrown into prison. There are some people whose days are ruined when it rains; Paul often received harsh physical abuse and still pressed on with his mission.

Paul and Silas while in prison still praised God and ministered to the other prisoners. One of my favorite prayers that a guy in a former church often used was "so that others see Thee in us." Remember Paul was dragged to the magistrates. He was falsely accused, beaten and thrown in prison. And Paul still maintained his demeanor.

What do you think Paul's success would have been had he lost his composure? Regardless of situation, leaders should continue to press forward. Even when the deck is stacked against you, you need to stay focused. Life is hard. If you quit when it gets tough you'll be a quitter your whole life.

Paul's main motivation was to know Christ (1 Cor. 15 and Phil 3:8). He had been chosen by the Lord and it was his hope and trust in Christ

– knowing that Christ is the ultimate wingman who would see him through. Christ will never leave us nor forsake us. (Heb 13:5)

Leaders always maintain their demeanor. When others see you calm during chaos, it will be easier for them to follow your example.

USING FACTS TO PERSUADE

As his custom was, Paul went into the synagogue, and on three Sabbath days he reasoned with them from the Scriptures, explaining and proving that the Christ had to suffer and rise from the dead. "This Jesus I am proclaiming to you is the Christ," he said. Some of the Jews were persuaded and joined Paul and Silas, as did a large number of God-fearing Greeks and not a few prominent women.

Acts 17:2-4

Paul and Silas continued their journey through Thessalonica. Paul's M-O ("Mode of Operation") when he first entered a city was to visit the synagogue, if there was one, and testify there. He would use Scripture (like all good pastors) and his own personal experience of Jesus to explain and prove the gospel. Ironically, the Jews were still waiting on their Messiah, and refused to acknowledge that Jesus was the Christ or Messiah.

Some people don't get that they don't get it. I will repeat this point often because it is so true. Paul did more than anyone to explain and prove the gospel. Paul never tried to change his message simply because there were still those who wouldn't believe. When you know you're right, you must continue to testify to the facts.

It is easy to bow to peer pressure but don't. Leaders have a duty to do what's right. Leaders are expected to use the facts and persuade. It's not your problem if those you are trying to persuade still don't agree with you. Some leaders have it easier than others when it comes to proving or disproving certain things based on experience, personality, charisma, knowledge, etc, but when you minimize emotion and stick to the facts you can't go wrong.

Even when one is right and has the facts, it is people's hearts that get in the way of truth. One can explain Christianity in depth and answer all the doubts – but some still will not believe because God has not opened their hearts (John 6:44) and because they suppress the truth. (Rom 1:18)

THE MASTER COMMUNICATOR

Paul then stood up in the meeting of the Areopagus and said: "Men of Athens! I see that in every way you are very religious. For as I walked around and looked carefully at your objects of worship, I even found an altar with this inscription: TO AN UNKNOWN GOD. Now what you worship as something unknown I am going to proclaim to you.

Acts 17:22-23

US Air Force Combat Controllers (my former career) are master communicators. They have a knack for delivering diverse issues to diverse groups of people and arriving at a favorable outcome using various forms of communication, particularly speech. Paul was a master communicator. Paul was very adept at taking a foreign, controversial, or heady topic and explaining it professionally and then garnering support. He was by no means 100% successful. However, I'll argue he was more successful at spreading the gospel (his mission) than anyone then or now, especially given what he was up against.

Paul was in Athens. In verse 21 we see these Athenians were men who did a lot of nothing - except talking about and listening to the latest ideas. Paul was given an opportunity to address the Areopagus. Now remember, the master communicator Paul was an expert at his message. Paul was an expert at delivering the gospel. And here we see Paul was an expert at analyzing his audience and communicated a 'new' idea with deftness.

Paul immediately built rapport by acknowledging they were very religious. He confirmed his careful study of their idols of worship. The Athenians had so many idols that they worshipped they even vainly had an altar to an unknown god just to ensure they didn't miss any. Paul used this fact to start to drive home his point…he was going to make known (vv 24-34) what they proclaimed as unknown.

A master communicator will analyze his audience to ensure not only the material is proper but the method of delivery fits the audience. More often than not, your message will be lost if one of these variables is inappropriate.

KNOW WHEN TO SAY WHEN

When Silas and Timothy came from Macedonia, Paul devoted himself exclusively to preaching, testifying to the Jews that Jesus was the Christ. But when the Jews opposed Paul and became abusive, he shook out his clothes in protest and said to them, "Your blood be on your own heads! I am clear of my responsibility. From now on I will go to the Gentiles."

Acts 18:5-6

In Corinth, Paul met with new friends Aquila and his wife Priscilla. Silas and Timothy also linked back up with Paul. Again the Jews opposed Paul and in protest he *shook out his clothes;* and declared "*your blood be on your own heads.*" Paul didn't stop testifying to the Jews nor did he stop visiting synagogues, but he let them know he was *clear of* his *responsibility.* We are responsible for discharging our duty and not responsible necessarily for how people respond.

Paul continued to use facts to persuade, but ignorant people don't know they're ignorant; so you need to know when to say when. Don't waste your time with unresponsive or obstructive people. If you know you've done the best you can, move on. You can fight another day.

Leaders aren't shy about telling it like it is. Too many times people avoid confrontation; not Paul. Leaders, as Paul often did, express their feelings. It doesn't mean you shouldn't be tactful or professional but you should still be direct.

Leaders know when to say when, as long as they are remaining true to their values, principles and mission.

LEADERS ALSO NEED REASSURANCE

One night the Lord spoke to Paul in a vision: "Do not be afraid; keep on speaking, do not be silent. For I am with you, and no one is going to attack and harm you, because I have many people in this city."

Acts 18:9-10

Paul was still in Corinth and had some success at this point in Scripture. One night the Lord spoke to him in a vision. In what had to be a great experience, Jesus gave Paul a pep talk.

Even strong leaders need reassurance. That can come from anywhere and often does. A friend and teammate of mine, Rick Barnes, once told me the higher you are the more bosses you have. I didn't realize it until I was a senior leader. When you're at a low rank or at an entry level position you truly only get guidance from your direct supervisor and maybe a level or two higher - maybe. Senior leaders have enormous demands from everyone below them and the senior leaders above them.

Some senior leaders are extraordinary at what they do and it appears they always got it going on. But what you don't see is that these guys get feedback also. They need it. There are times when doubt may set in or at least anxiety or trepidation and they need a course correction. Or maybe they are doing well and the positive feedback will not only motivate the leader but also resonate throughout the organization.

Some times when you're the man, it takes a bigger man to say "I've got your back." "Keep doing what you're doing." "You're doing great." I've known great men who reported directly to Combatant Commanders, the Secretary of Defense, and the President. These men have enormous responsibility, and since they are human, they sometimes need reassurance.

Reassurance can also come from peers and those below the leader. If you don't know how you're doing you probably have communication problems in your organization. Think about it, if you're truly doing well or truly screwing up, you'll hear about it.

Senior Leaders need reassurance. If you're in a position to give it, do so.

LEADERS ARE TRAINERS

But some of them became obstinate; they refused to believe and publicly maligned the Way. So Paul left them. He took the disciples with him and had discussions daily in the lecture hall of Tyrannus. This went on for two years, so that all the Jews and Greeks who lived in the province of Asia heard the word of the Lord.

Acts 19:9-10

Paul was on his third missionary journey. Now in Ephesus, in verse 8 he spoke boldly in the synagogue for three months. Then in verse 9 they refused to believe, so Paul had daily discussions in the lecture hall of Tyrannus for two years. For two years Paul preached the word. For two years Paul trained the young believers.

In the movie *Remember the Titans*, one of the other coaches looked at Denzel Washington's playbook and said something like "that's a pretty small playbook." Denzel's reply was "I only run six plays, but it's like Novocain, give it time and it always works." Paul had one message: the gospel. And for two years in Ephesus Paul spoke the gospel.

I don't know how many *all* was but all the Jews and Greeks in the province of Asia heard the gospel. Paul was nothing if he wasn't persistent and consistent. Leaders must be persistent and consistent.

Leaders are trainers. As a trainer you must realize your trainees will be at various levels of experience and knowledge. You can't go to "Gospel

404" if a new convert has not graduated "Gospel 101." Paul spoke to, preached to, and trained the Ephesians.

Leaders should always ensure their organizations are training. Whether they are actually delivering the training or not, at least they ensure it's getting done. Regardless of experience level, leaders and trainers should drill the "basics" over and over again. Paul drilled the basics.

LEADERS MAY BE FALSELY ATTACKED

And you see and hear how this fellow Paul has convinced and led astray large numbers of people here in Ephesus and in practically the whole province of Asia. He says that man-made gods are no gods at all.

Acts 19:26

The riot in Ephesus is a great story in Acts 19:23-41. In Ephesus they worshipped the Greek goddess Artemis. A pagan silversmith named Demetrius had been making a tidy living fashioning graven images of Artemis, and was quickly realizing that with all these Christian conversions he and his fellow merchants were losing business fast. Apparently their wares weren't selling as well after Paul arrived. After all, once people got to realizing there is only one true and living God, the demand for silver idols is bound to drop! So, Demetrius and his buddies started an up-roar. Interestingly, despite an angry mob and a massive riot, the rule of law prevailed.

Demetrius falsely accused Paul of leading astray large numbers of people and 'blamed' Paul for stating manmade gods were no gods at all. Paul did lead a large number of people to Christ. And Paul was right: manmade gods are not gods at all.

Leaders may be falsely attacked. You will not make 100% of the people happy. You must realize that, if you are effective, you will receive criticism from some. To prove this, I only need to tell you what happened to Jesus. The greatest leader of all time was crucified.

Leaders are by their very nature out front. It makes no sense, but there are people who don't like change. There are people that don't like it when others are successful. There are people that will attack (even if they're wrong) if they feel their way is being infringed upon. Because leaders oftentimes find themselves in the middle of these situations they may be falsely attacked.

LEADERS CONTINUE THEIR WORK DESPITE THE TIME

On the first day of the week we came together to break bread. Paul spoke to the people and, because he intended to leave the next day, kept on talking until midnight.

Acts 20:7

Paul was speaking to believers in Troas. The first part of the verse pertains to the Sabbath. But I want you to take note of the latter part of the verse. The latter part says that Paul intended to leave *the next day* - yet, Paul continued to preach and teach. Sleep must wait when the job needs to get done. Time is a scarce resource; some use it more wisely than others. Paul even spoke so late into the night that a young man named Eutychus fell asleep while sitting in a window and fell to his death. Paul of course brought him back to life and little else is spoken about the young man.

Leaders get the job done regardless of the time of day. Regardless of deadline, time available or any other obstacles, leaders press on to get their task done. Too many people are influenced by time, or the perceived need to rest, or external factors, or just plain excuses why they don't get done what needs to get done.

Paul's priority was preaching the gospel. He tried to maximize his time. Leaders try to maximize their time whenever possible. There is a lot to be said about leaders who appear to always have enough time to do everything.

While I was serving in the Air Force, and even more so now, I hear "I'm so busy." Or "I didn't get it done because I'm so busy." I confirmed in virtually every circumstance the person was not a true leader. A true leader makes no excuses for anything, including making excuses about not having enough time.

SELFLESS SACRIFICE

I only know that in every city the Holy Spirit warns me that prison and hardships are facing me. However, I consider my life worth nothing to me, if only I may finish the race and complete the task the Lord Jesus has given me—the task of testifying to the gospel of God's grace.

Acts 20:23-24

Paul was in Miletus on his way back to Jerusalem toward the end of his third missionary journey. He sent for the elders from the church of Ephesus (note: he was constantly teaching). Then in verses 18-22 he gave another wonderful testimony.

Paul was Jesus' instrument to the Gentiles (Acts 9:15). Paul was totally focused on finishing the race and completing the task given him by the Lord Jesus. Paul knew he constantly faced threats and hardships, yet this did not stop him…ever. He even said he considered his life nothing except to testify the gospel (Acts 20:24)

Paul was the epitome of selfless sacrifice. Why was Paul faced with so much hardship? I'm not sure. Whatever the reason, it was all part of God's plan. And Paul knew it was all part of God's plan, and he gave Him all the glory.

Without Paul, Christianity may not have survived that tough first century. Without Paul, Christianity would not be where it is today. Paul was selfless. One of the reasons he had so much success despite the innumerable hardships was because of his selflessness. Most people would have quit under similar circumstances.

A true leader sacrifices his personal comfort for the common goal. A true leader sacrifices his personal gain for team gain. Paul sacrificed everything to testify the gospel and glorify God.

CONSTANTLY MENTOR UPCOMING LEADERS

Keep watch over yourselves and all the flock of which the Holy Spirit has made you overseers. Be shepherds of the church of God, which he bought with his own blood. I know that after I leave, savage wolves will come in among you and will not spare the flock.

Acts 20:28-29

Paul told the Ephesian elders he would never see them again. Paul probably knew what lay in wait not only for him but for these upcoming leaders, and he wanted to give them a pep talk of sorts. Paul knew the value of this constant mentoring the next generation of leaders.

Young leaders are at danger of losing confidence. Obviously, due to their inexperience and lack of maturity, their progress may get cut short. Paul had a huge list of leaders he initiated, grew, and developed. Without leaders at every level, no organization will grow or become successful.

Paul used an analogy these men would understand. He used words like *flock, overseers, shepherds,* and *savage wolves.* He reiterated how the Holy Spirit made them the overseers of the church *bought with* the *blood* of Jesus; definitely a hearty reminder. He warned them of the savage wolves that would come.

Leaders and mentors need to constantly build confidence, but they also need to speak directly and with truth. Leaders want it straight. There isn't a need to soft-soap something, and Paul definitely was direct with these men.

LEAD BY EXAMPLE

You yourselves know that these hands of mine have supplied my own needs and the needs of my companions. In everything I did, I showed you that by this kind of hard work we must help the weak, remembering the words the Lord Jesus himself said: 'It is more blessed to give than to receive.'"

Acts 20:34-35

Paul is about to leave the elders from the church in Ephesus while in Miletus. There are numerous lessons in these two verses. As an apostle Paul had a right to be taken care of by the Church. However, he took care of himself. Sure there are a lot of examples while in prison and other places Paul was tended to. However, Paul led by example in everything he did.

Leaders shouldn't have to be taken care of. They should pull their own weight, so to speak. Paul was a tentmaker and used his trade to provide for himself. He reminded the elders of the value of this and other hard work. He also reiterated that his and their hard work must help the weak, a timeless tenet of the Church.

Leaders who garner the most respect (there are quite a few other reasons why) often lead by example. Especially in environments like the military and team athletics, environments that are labor intensive, leaders who are physically doing everything the men are doing are normally more respected. Now this doesn't take away from the fact that each person in an organization has a specific role. For example, a leader shouldn't be emptying trash when bigger picture things need to be done.

Leading by example can mean something tangible like physical labor, or it can mean simply being a man whose character is above reproach. Leading by example means regardless of where you're at or what you're doing, your actions and character must exceed the standards of your organization.

A HIGHER CALLING

The following night the Lord stood near Paul and said, "Take courage! As you have testified about me in Jerusalem, so you must also testify in Rome."

Acts 23:11

After Paul's return to Jerusalem he spent some time with the brothers including James. Then some Jews stirred up the crowd and they seized him, bent on killing him. While they were beating him, the commander of the Roman troops appeared and took Paul into custody, probably saving his life. Paul then asked to speak to the crowd, and again retold his testimony of his conversion and his mission to the Gentiles.

Again the crowd began an up-roar, and the commander had Paul taken into the barracks. He assumed Paul must have done something wrong, and was about to have him flogged and questioned. Paul tactfully informed the commander that he was a Roman (and that what the commander was about to do was illegal). Paul and the commander compared how each became a Roman: Paul by birth the commander by bribe.

To get to the bottom of this, the commander called for the chief priests and all the Sanhedrin and had Paul stand before them. In Acts 23:2 Paul gets struck in the mouth shortly after he begins his testimony. He then had a very direct and impassioned engagement with the high priest and some others. Paul reiterated his belief in the Resurrection which deftly pit the Pharisees and Sadducees against each other. Again there was a great uproar and the commander, afraid for Paul's safety, took him again into the barracks.

Paul had completed three missionary journeys consisting of thousands and thousands of miles. He had successes in large chunks of the known world. Yet still, a lot of Jews (especially the leaders) continuously tried to stop his ministry. But in a simple statement, "*Take courage!*" Jesus told Paul he had a higher calling…*to testify in Rome.* Again this was all part of God's plan.

Relatively speaking Jesus visited and spent time in a very small part of the world. His impact was beyond measure. Jesus commissioned Paul (and with the help of the Holy Spirit) to preach the gospel to the Gentiles and the center of this was Rome. Jesus knew Paul not only needed to testify to the Roman population, of which one fifth to one third were slaves, but also to its leaders.

Paul was about to go to the figurative center of the world: Rome. But first this higher calling had stops with Felix, Festus and Agrippa.

TRUE LEADERS DON'T SEEK MAN'S FAVOR

When Paul was called in, Tertullus presented his case before Felix: "We have enjoyed a long period of peace under you, and your foresight has brought about reforms in this nation. Everywhere and in every way, most excellent Felix, we acknowledge this with profound gratitude.

Acts 24:2-3

Paul was on trial before the governor Felix. The Jews had their high priest, some of the elders, and a lawyer named Tertullus bring their charges against Paul. Tertullus immediately started to kiss up to Felix. Felix probably enjoyed it and was looking to get what he could get out of the situation. Tertullus laid out their false charges against Paul. When it was Paul's turn to speak, he again used facts to prove his innocence.

True leaders always act professionally. Tertullus appeared to try to win Felix's favor by a little schmoozing. All good leaders can be savvy, and "work" a room but a true leader will never "kiss up." You lose credibility when you kiss up. Kissing up shows you don't have spine. It shows you can't stand tall on your own. Most true leaders can immediately spot a kiss up and will instantly think poorly of the person and it will wreck any sort of credibility he has.

Those that have a sense of self-importance will enjoy and enable the kissing up. Don't be that guy. If you're a leader don't let it happen to you and don't let it happen in your organization. It doesn't have any real positive impact, except to make a fake leader feel good about himself. In my experience, kiss ups normally got put in their place. Ironically, weak organizations have more than their fair share of kiss ups.

Men of character, men of substance, don't kiss up nor do they tolerate kiss ups.

HOW FAR ARE YOU WILLING TO GO

Then Paul answered, "Why are you weeping and breaking my heart? I am ready not only to be bound, but also to die in Jerusalem for the name of the Lord Jesus."

Acts 21:13

Paul finally left Miletus and made his way by ship to Phoenicia. While in Caesarea, Paul stayed with Philip. Agabus came from Judea and prophesized Paul's capture in Jerusalem. All the people there pleaded with Paul not to go to Jerusalem. But obviously it was God's will and that's what Paul did.

Once converted, Paul was as focused as anyone toward accomplishing his mission. Paul willingly laid his life on the line. There are leaders today that barely have a pulse in order to 'not rock the boat.' Paul, however, was willing to die in the name of Jesus.

How far are you willing to go? I'm not sure I'm willing to die to accomplish my mission of *Positively Influencing Lives*. Most of us aren't willing to die; nor are we even expected to. But truly, how far are you willing to go?

Leaders face many obstacles. A leader willing to go farther than anyone else will have an unstoppable organization.

STAYING ON MESSAGE

Several days later Felix came with his wife Drusilla, who was a Jewess. He sent for Paul and listened to him as he spoke about faith in Christ Jesus. As Paul discoursed on righteousness, self-control and the judgment to come, Felix was afraid and said, "That's enough for now! You may leave. When I find it convenient, I will send for you." At the same time he was hoping that Paul would offer him a bribe, so he sent for him frequently and talked with him.

Acts 24:24-26

In verse 22 Felix adjourned the proceedings and ordered the centurion to keep Paul under guard. In verse 27 we're told Paul was kept under Felix's control for two years. For two years Paul was sent for frequently and preached the gospel to Felix and his wife Drusilla. For two years Paul testified about Jesus and His teachings. For two years Paul stayed on message.

It's remarkable to truly think about what Paul endured. I would venture to say a lot of Christians today (myself included) could not measure up to Paul's persistence and faith. But persistence and faith defined Paul. Felix hoped for a bribe, it never came. What did come? The gospel, that's what!

Paul preached and taught everywhere and at every opportunity he had. True leaders stay on message. Inconsistency, lack of dedication, wishy-washiness (yes, it's a word), and indecisiveness hamper so many leaders.

True leaders stay on message no matter what.

ALL THE WAY

If, however, I am guilty of doing anything deserving death, I do not refuse to die. But if the charges brought against me by these Jews are not true, no one has the right to hand me over to them. I appeal to Caesar!"

Acts 25:11

Festus succeeded Felix. When in Jerusalem the chief priests and Jewish leaders again presented their charges to Festus against Paul. They wanted Festus to transfer Paul to Jerusalem since they were preparing to ambush him and kill him. Festus told them to come to Caesarea if they wanted to press their charges. Again Paul found himself on trial facing false charges.

Paul laid it out in verse 11. He pronounced his innocence. Although Paul did not *refuse to die* for Jesus, he reminded Festus the charges were false and said no one had the right to turn him over to the Jews. He *appealed to Caesar*! I am not sure if Paul had Acts 23:11 in mind when Jesus said Paul would testify in Rome but, *"I appeal to Caesar!"* guaranteed he was on his way. As a Roman citizen Paul had certain rights. At times his rights were countered and at times he ensured he used them. Paul was in the world, but not of it. He was shrewd as a snake and as innocent as a dove. (Matthew 10:16)

In one verse Paul went all the way: pronounced his innocence; squashed the accusations; acknowledged his willingness to die for the cause; gave Festus a face full of facts; and appealed to Caesar.

When necessary, true leaders go all the way. "All the way" is a matter of perspective, and oftentimes it won't mean a willingness to die, or appeal to the President or Supreme Court. But it will mean "all the way" in the environment you're in, and to those that know, know what it means.

THE POWER OF PUBLIC SPEECH

Then Agrippa said to Paul, "You have permission to speak for yourself." So Paul motioned with his hand and began his defense: "King Agrippa, I consider myself fortunate to stand before you today as I make my defense against all the accusations of the Jews, and especially so because you are well acquainted with all the Jewish customs and controversies. Therefore, I beg you to listen to me patiently.

Acts 26:1-3

Paul had worked his way up the chain of command: now King Agrippa. Festus literally did not know what to do. So he asked Agrippa for help. Festus gave Agrippa the details of the case. At the start of chapter 26 Agrippa gave Paul a chance to speak. And boy did Paul use that opportunity.

Look at these words in verse 3: *well acquainted, Jewish customs and controversies, listen,* and *patiently*. What a master orator. In a few words he masterfully laid out an articulate introduction. He established some common ground. *Controversies,* what does that mean? I'm not sure, but it appears Paul knew Agrippa would know. He told Agrippa he was going to defend *all* of *the accusations*. And as chapter 26 tells us "all" meant all and Agrippa needed to listen patiently.

In my study of leaders, all great leaders have the power of public speech. Show me someone who doesn't like, is afraid of, or avoids public speech and I'll show you someone with limited leadership impact. Paul knew the value of public speech and he was always ready to deliver the gospel. Paul had rehearsed his speech dozens of times before. And like all good leaders, this particular speech, this succinct summary of his life, mission, and purpose had been carefully crafted in his mind long before it was needed. Effective public speech is highly intentional. Good leaders make it look easy, but it never is. Will powerful public speech guarantee a favorable outcome for a leader? No. But I have definitely seen a lack of powerful public speech hamper, if not totally diminish, a favorable outcome. I'm not saying that's right or wrong, I'm saying that's just the way it is.

God was so powerful through Paul that in verse 28 it appeared Agrippa almost became a believer, *"do you think in such a short time… you can persuade me…?"* To become better at anything takes practice and that includes public speech. Leaders need to seek opportunities to practice public speaking. There are a few ways you can be considered a "good" or even a "great" public speaker. One: be a master of your material and two: be a master at delivery.

BE BOLD

Boldly and without hindrance he preached the kingdom of God and taught about the Lord Jesus Christ.

Acts 28:31

This is the last verse in Acts. Paul was under house arrest and for two years *he boldly and without hindrance preached*. He was in Rome (just as God had stated he would be), the capital of the Roman Empire, and he was able to preach and teach.

We don't know how many people Paul delivered the gospel to but we do know his actions had history-changing effect. God put Paul in Rome to minister to the Gentiles and he did so, even though he was under house arrest. In verse 16 we see that Paul was guarded even though he lived in his own house that he had to provide for. It appears a guard was there 24/7. So while Paul was preaching and teaching obviously the guards were hearing this and bringing back this testimony to their fellow soldiers.

Regardless of situation, but especially at those critical times, a leader must be bold. Paul appeared to have so much stacked against him but it never stopped him. Whether faced with death, impossible odds, unpopularity, danger, whatever could be construed as a negative outcome, true leaders are bold in their actions and in their speech.

RESTATEMENT OF MISSION

God, whom I serve with my whole heart in preaching the gospel of his Son, is my witness how constantly I remember you

Romans 1:9

Paul had not been to Rome at this time. He wanted to and later in Romans he stated his plans to visit Rome as well as Spain. At the time of the writing Paul was probably on his third missionary journey. The book of Romans is a phenomenal book of pure theological doctrine and a great testament of the gospel. This letter was written to the Christians at Rome.

Paul restated his mission, commissioned by Jesus, to the Romans. There is value in restating your mission to those who don't know or need to be reminded. Paul had not been to Rome, someone else established the church there. Paul wanted to remind the Romans of his mission as well as provide some praise, *how I constantly remember you.*

A true leader keeps his mission foremost in his mind and actions. Also, he needs to drill home his common philosophies and principals. Once you find the handful of key values, principals, goals, truths, etc - keep hammering them home. Once you've established a foundation, you can build from there, but to always keep building onto the strong foundation and mission is as basic as it gets.

REWARDED FOR WHAT YOU DO

God "will give to each person according to what he has done."
                                                    Romans 2:6

This is a great verse. This verse is a baseline teaching for all Christians. It's also expressed in Psalm 62:12, Proverbs 24:12, and Matthew 16:27. And the evidence of *what he has done* will be how we glorified God as well as how we treated and served Jesus' brothers and sisters.

However, in a secular world I totally appreciate being rewarded for doing well. I also appreciate the reciprocal. Leaders need to ensure they reward those who exceed the standards. While a Combat Controller, then a Financial Advisor, and now a Bank Manager I was and am in an environment that rewards success. My environment doesn't, nor should it, reward mediocrity.

In my former profession as Financial Advisor, good guys finished first. The profession had lots of examples of dishonorable people that had the gall to call themselves *trusted* advisors. I knew one specifically (not with my company), that had a reputation amongst many for being a liar. I even personally experienced this man in action. As for myself, I will ensure I exceed the standards of character, competence and commitment. All my relationships are, and will be, built on trust, and I have been, and will be rewarded for that.

Good leaders will be rewarded. You shouldn't be in any environment for the rewards, but if you do well you'll be recognized. As a leader, do not allow those who don't measure up to receive the accolades deserving of your best guys.

WHAT TO DO

To those who by persistence in doing good seek glory, honor and immortality, he will give eternal life.

Romans 2:7

A former commander of mine, Colonel Jim Oeser, used to coach the Air Force Academy wrestling team. He told us that between periods he would tell his men "do" one thing and "don't" do one thing. More than that, the guy won't remember.

Leadership, supervision, training, most everything comes down to some basics in whatever environment you're in. Once you know those basics be consistent in hitting them hard.

Whether they are simple organization rules or complex instructions, there are basic "Do's" to keep reminding folks of. It needs to be at the subconscious level.

One of the things I remind my daughter of almost every day is "Always try your best." As we drive to school I'll ask, "What do you always do?" She'll respond "Try your best."

WHAT NOT TO DO

But for those who are self-seeking and who reject the truth and follow evil, there will be wrath and anger.

Romans 2:8

Just as there are "Do's" there are also "Don'ts." It seems there are a lot of don'ts in our world. Maybe because life brings a lot of opportunity for someone to do something wrong and the next thing you have is a binder full of regulations stating all the don'ts.

Don'ts are important especially when it pertains to extremely important issues like life or death, physical danger, someone's life savings, possibly going to jail, or being on the front page with the headline "Under Investigation."

The direct opposite to the "do" I remind my daughter is: "What do you never do?" She'll respond "Never quit." Pretty simple huh?

CHARACTER REVEALED

Not only so, but we also rejoice in our sufferings, because we know that suffering produces perseverance; perseverance, character; and character, hope.

Romans 5:3-4

Paul wrote that when believers suffer they develop perseverance. Perseverance will then deepen their character, and this deepened, tested character will result in hope that God will see them through. Character is sometimes made and built upon during adversity; character is *always* revealed during adversity.

Men of character have normally been honed through years of discipline. You can see this in military environments especially in a special operations environment. You can also see this in an athletic environment. But this is also revealed in our Christian maturation.

True leaders are men of character. This character is developed through years of practice and study in their profession. Show me a leader who hasn't suffered or dealt with set backs, losses, failure, defeat and I'll show you an under developed leader. Now I didn't say you have to be a screw up to be a leader. I mean a leader who has never failed or encountered obstacles is either not being honest with themselves or not pushing the limits. A leader's character is revealed during adversity.

Suffering produces perseverance. Perseverance produces character. And character produces hope. The adage "been there, done that" is very appropriate. Who would you rather be with: a leader that has innumerable experiences in similar and disparate situations, or a leader whose experience is based on what they learned in a book or a school?

Leaders are going to deal with adversity. Without adversity we wouldn't need leaders. Those who have many years of perseverance and an inner core full of character will lead their organizations regardless of what the adversities are.

PREDESTINED

For those God foreknew he also predestined to be conformed to the likeness of his Son, that he might be the firstborn among many brothers. And those he predestined, he also called; those he called, he also justified; those he justified, he also glorified.

Romans 8:29-30

It's wonderful knowing what lays ahead of us believers. We are predestined; God knew us before we were born. He chose us; we didn't choose Him. We are called to do His will. We are saved by grace through faith. These are all Christian truths. "Glorified," in Romans 8:30, means eternal life in His presence. The word is used as if it's a done deal.

Since we are predestined, true leaders know this and attempt to live and lead as Christ-like as possible. This has been extremely hard, and in some situations near impossible for me. As my faith matures I realize it is all about Him. Once you realize that, as a Christian and as a leader you start to act differently: better, more positive, more genuine.

Our victory is in heaven with Jesus. Our victory is now. But before He comes or we go, we need to use our God-given gifts to do His will. A true leader has such a phenomenal ability to build people up, to inspire, and to positively influence lives.

How awesome is it to know we're called by the Lord. I don't act as humble as I should in that knowledge. I do try to positively influence lives and do so in a manner that would glorify God.

LEADERS GROW

Do not conform any longer to the pattern of this world, but be transformed by the renewing of your mind. Then you will be able to test and approve what God's will is—his good, pleasing and perfect will.

Romans 12:2

Believers are constantly being renewed from the inside out. The key is the mind. This controls the attitudes, actions, and feelings. The more you are in tune with God's will; the more able you are to achieve it.

Just as a Christian should mature, a leader must mature or continue to grow. How do we "renew our minds?" We renew through reading, watching, listening, formal education, etc. Regardless of venue, the more you learn, the more you realize how much you don't know. Through this learning you will gain knowledge and skills. Just as importantly, you will develop resilience, patience, tolerance and understanding. These are crucial leadership traits that allow you to relate to, and communicate with others better.

Leaders constantly seek to better themselves. Leaders constantly seek to grow.

USE YOUR GIFTS

We have different gifts, according to the grace given us. If a man's gift is prophesying, let him use it in proportion to his faith.

Romans 12:6

God has given believers certain gifts for His spiritual service. In verses 6 – 8 Paul lists seven possible gifts according to God's grace. Christians must use their gifts to further God's kingdom. It appears that a lot of immature believers don't know what their gifts are; or don't realize what they are; or aren't looking to find out what their gifts are. But once you realize what it is or they are, you need to use them to bring glory to God.

A true leader is aware of his gifts. They can take the form of inspiration, motivation, organization, vision, public speech, competence and plenty of others. A true leader uses his gift or gifts for the betterment of his organization.

HONOR ONE ANOTHER

Be devoted to one another in brotherly love. Honor one another above yourselves.

Romans 12:10

This is one of our Christian tenets. We are to love each other as Jesus loved us. A true leader loves what he does. He also loves his people. If you are truly fulfilling a leadership role you know that it takes people to complete the mission, goal, or task.

You cannot be the most effective without loving, honoring or respecting your teammates. Honor one another. We do this by always respecting others. We keep our word, we keep information shared with us confidential, we do not gossip, we lend a hand when needed, we praise in public, we champion our people, we give the credit to those deserving, and we simply adhere to the Golden Rule.

Besides honoring one another we should also live "with" honor. Always tell the truth, do the right thing even when no one is looking, stand up for what is right, don't make what you do seem like a big deal, accept praise professionally, and exude character above reproach.

DO THE RIGHT THING

Do not repay anyone evil for evil. Be careful to do what is right in the eyes of everybody.

Romans 12:17

Leaders are always being watched and most people are looking at "what to do." A true leader is a good example. You definitely lead by example; make that example good. Don't be a leader that leads the wrong way.

True leaders do the right thing. Even if conventional wisdom says something not right would be the better accepted thing to do; strive to the do the right thing anyway, at all times.

LIVE AT PEACE WITH EVERYONE

If it is possible, as far as it depends on you, live at peace with everyone.
Romans 12:18

This is one of my favorite verses of scripture. The first time it really hit home was when I read one of Billy Graham's daily columns from the newspaper. I also used it in a message I delivered in January 2008. My message title was "You Reap What You Sow." I used Galatians 6:1-10 for the meat of the message. Part of my message described my own walk up to that point. Billy Graham's column was about some guy who was angry at his mother and the hurt she had caused him. When I look back at those times where I was not as effective as I could have been, it was never because of lack of competence, or lack of motivation, or lack of organization, or lack of knowing my mission; it was due to not being at peace with someone.

I try my best to truly live at peace with everyone. Not too long ago I was always at it with someone or vice versa. Once you realize no one really wins an argument you give up trying to win all your arguments. Do I still have disagreements? Absolutely, but I try not to be disagreeable. I strive to live at peace with everyone, regardless if they're believers or unbelievers.

The first way to live at peace is to actually become more mature, and *be* at peace - be more secure in your manhood. I've spent countless, valuable hours in the past nitpicking or talking junk about people. Once the issue of insecurity is dealt with, most of your problems with people will disappear, because the problems won't matter as much. Another way to live at peace is to bite your tongue. Think about it: if you actually forced yourself to say nothing, or only responded positively to others you'll find yourself in far fewer stressful environments.

And the final way, although you need to ensure you've done everything within your ability not to get here, is staying away from a person. This virtually guarantees you won't find yourself at odds with him. It's amazing how at peace I am, when I'm not around those that spend most of their day at odds with everything and/or everyone.

THE BOTTOM LINE

Love does no harm to its neighbor. Therefore love is the fulfillment of the law.

Romans 13:10

Yet another great verse of scripture. Paul at times was confusing and hard to understand (II Peter 3:15, 16) he also was straight and to the point. I love this verse: *love is the fulfillment of the law.* Jesus is love. Love is the fulfillment of the law. Jesus fulfilled the law. This does not mean the Old Testament is not important. This does not mean the law was not important. This does not mean Paul stopped being a Jew nor stopped adhering to their customs. But Paul as succinctly as he could, gave the bottom line to the law.

Christianity has some bottom line tenets: those facts that are not debatable. A leader at times needs to ensure his organization knows the bottom line. The Bottom Line is the #1 critical issue, and to repeat the "bottom line" often ensures it's adhered to or sought after. The bottom line is also a communication technique. A lot of people are too verbose or wordy. The bottom line breaks it down and cuts to the chase.

I've been told I write and speak in bullet points. Maybe I do. I like to think from a "bottom line" focus at times. For example when you are discussing an issue in person, over the phone, in a briefing, on email, or virtually over any medium a "bottom line" focus ensures the person or the audience knows the main point. It sort of says "this is what I 'really' need you to know."

Use "the bottom line" when you are truly putting the #1 critical issue on the table and you need everyone to know it's THE bottom line. Paul was the master at it and in this verse says it all.

BE DIRECT

I have written you quite boldly on some points, as if to remind you of them again, because of the grace God gave me

Romans 15:15

Paul started to wrap up Romans. This is arguably the greatest "theological" book in the Bible. Paul reminded the Roman believers of the points he had boldly written not because they didn't know, but because he was reiterating his Christ-given mission. Paul was bold throughout the New Testament. He wrote boldly so there is no doubt of his testimony or the message of the gospel.

I can't count how many so-called leaders acted without boldness, and consequently had little or no impact or success. A commander early in my career would not hold men accountable. He would allow men to get away with things that deserved discipline. After a while, you realized we were an undisciplined unit. A true leader is bold and acts boldly. I don't mean a leader needs to run over people or be a "tough guy" for the sake of boldness, I mean he needs to stand his ground, be direct, be straightforward, be decisive, be confident, able to say "yes" when the whole world is saying "no", or say "no" when the whole world is saying "yes."

A true leader has a spine. I was stationed with a Captain who at that time was a flight commander. He became aware of a discipline issue and quickly squared it away even when his position (the right one by the way) was unpopular. He deftly took point on the issue and ultimately his recommendations were agreed with by the commander and the issue was professionally resolved.

Tell me like it is. Be truthful. Don't sugarcoat. Be up front. Be bold. Be direct. I can't stand men who hem and haw. I can't stand men who waffle. I can't stand men who always have an excuse. I can't stand men who can never make a decision. I can't stand men who easily change a decision.

A bold leader knows his mission, knows what he wants to say, knows what he needs to do, and does it.

BE ON GUARD

I urge you, brothers, to watch out for those who cause divisions and put obstacles in your way that are contrary to the teaching you have learned. Keep away from them.

Romans 16:17

In this last chapter of Romans, Paul gave his personal greetings to a lot of his friends, fellow workers, and brothers. He cautioned the Romans to be on guard against those that are bound to disrupt his teaching and the gospel. He instructed them to *keep away from them.*

As much as I try, I have yet to find an environment totally void of conflict. I am not sure it's possible here on Earth. I struggle with doing the right thing as I know God would want me to do it. I try to be a "good" Christian. Even though not of the world, we are in it and we need to be on our guard against unbelievers that will push false doctrines, false teaching, blasphemy, and lies. We need to be aware of them and avoid them.

It's totally ironic that we KNOW the truth, yet there are still others bent on trying to destroy the truth. Don't ask me why. That's just the way it is. I've been asked based on my experience in a bunch of foreign lands, "Why do certain people or certain religions act the way they do?" My response will normally be a series of questions: "Do you believe in the gospel?" (yes), "Do you believe Jesus is the Son of God and died for our sins?" (yes), "Do you believe nonbelievers will spend eternity in a fiery lake?" (again the answer is yes), "Do you believe God will reward believers with eternal life?" (yes). Well amazingly, there are those that don't believe any of this, yet they believe their way is truth.

A true leader knows obstacles will get in his way. Prepare for them. Then, either overpower them or avoid them. A true leader will maintain the right way. He won't succumb to peer-pressure or the easy road. A true leader will press through and bring his followers with him.

ESTABLISHING AUTHORITY

Paul, called to be an apostle of Christ Jesus by the will of God, and our brother Sosthenes,

1 Corinthians 1:1

Paul used this similar opening in most of his letters. There was contradiction being raised by some Corinthians as to Paul's authority. Paul let there be no doubt he was an apostle of Christ; he was Jesus' messenger. Not only was Paul an apostle of Christ he was fulfilling his duty *by the will of God*.

Paul's authority was constantly challenged. He spent an inordinate amount of time defending his apostleship. And he made sure everyone knew this apostleship was commissioned personally by Jesus. He was not vindictive about it; he was merely being truthful and direct in his own Paul-esque way.

Leaders don't often have to establish their authority. In most environments leaders are identified as the leaders. In environments where you find yourself challenged it is necessary to establish your authority. Remember personal power is better than position power. At those times you do it as Paul did: truthfully and directly. No one living has the authority of Jesus as the apostles did, but all leaders have certain "levels" of authority.

True leaders' authority comes from proven experience.

PERFECTLY UNITED

I appeal to you, brothers, in the name of our Lord Jesus Christ, that all of you agree with one another so that there may be no divisions among you and that you may be perfectly united in mind and thought.

1 Corinthians 1:10

There was a lot of dissension in the church at Corinth. There were a lot of wrongs that needed to be righted in Corinth. Some were following Christ's teachings, others were following Paul's and others were adhering to Peter's. Christians have certain tenets that are inarguable. Jesus Christ is the Son of God and was crucified, died and resurrected to take away the sins of the world and allow eternal life to those that believe. Paul made sure his gospel was focused *in the name of our Lord Jesus Christ*.

Paul wanted unity in Corinth. He taught those unifying themes in his travels and writings. These included, but weren't limited to, love, harmony, and salvation. It's impossible to be "perfectly united" in anything of this world; but Paul wanted the Corinthians and us to strive for this state of spiritual and doctrinal unity.

A leader wants his organization to be united on all core values and principles. A true leader knows there is value in our differences and diversity but an organization cannot reach perfect unity without everyone on the same page when it comes to those critical issues.

BUILD ON THE FOUNDATION

By the grace God has given me, I laid a foundation as an expert builder, and someone else is building on it. But each one should be careful how he builds.

1 Corinthians 3:10

The *foundation* is Jesus Christ. Paul, as well as Apollos and others, taught the gospel to the Corinthians. But Paul warned against a false teacher. Christians first and foremost focus on Christ. Antichrists say Jesus is not the Son of God. The foundation for us all has, is, and always will be Jesus. This was Paul's gospel. He *laid a foundation*. On this foundation additional teaching and experience should be built. It appeared a false teacher was negatively impacting this.

A true leader builds on the foundation. First he lays the foundation. That foundation is the critical principles of an organization. These are the inarguable points that a leader does not bend on. These are the inarguable lessons a leader continuously hammers home. These are the inarguable facts that an organization is built upon.

We need to ensure the "good" foundation that we laid is not hampered or impacted by those that are preaching false truths. We cannot build on a foundation that has started weakly. We must build a strong foundation and continue to build self-sustaining layers. However, each layer in an organization is dependent upon the layer above and below them.

I will always ensure those critical few principles will be championed across my organization. If that is the case, our foundation is strong and we can further build additional strong layers. If that foundation is weak, our organization will be weak.

A true leader builds and maintains a strong foundation in an organization.

FAITHFUL SERVICE

Now it is required that those who have been given a trust must prove faithful.

1 Corinthians 4:2

Paul is referring to the faithful service of those entrusted *with the secret things of God.* (vs 1) God has, through His Holy Spirit and Word, revealed His wisdom and His gospel to those that believe. Those men who were entrusted to be Apostles (as was Paul's case), or those entrusted to lead, teach, or minister in any capacity, must take this revelation and faithfully serve.

We *must prove faithful* in our service to Jesus. Paul was the epitome of faithful service. When you consider the fact that his beginnings involved being a fierce persecutor of Jesus' followers, and then went to being Jesus' most ardent servant, you must conclude that Paul's faithful service never wavered.

Leaders are entrusted to serve their organizations as well as those members in that organization. True leaders serve faithfully. *Those who have been given a trust must prove faithful.* True leaders have an awesome responsibility to serve their organizations. Those that do it well propel their organizations and force multiply their organizations.

When followers can trust a leader and see that he is a faithful servant, they will exceed any standard, overcome any obstacle, or deal with any opposition put in their way.

LEADERS ARE ALWAYS ON DISPLAY

For it seems to me that God has put us apostles on display at the end of the procession, like men condemned to die in the arena. We have been made a spectacle to the whole universe, to angels as well as to men.

1 Corinthians 4:9

Here is a visual of a Roman general leading a procession of victors with captives at the end; men condemned to die either as a gladiator or against wild beasts. Paul referred to the *apostles* being brought in to fight to the death as the *whole universe* looked on.

Paul knew how Christ was dehumanized, and humiliatingly paraded to His death, and yet he likened the life of Christ's servants the same way. Servants of Christ always have and always will face persecution, obstacles, ridicule, and opposition. That's why we must persevere. Christ told us to *be of good cheer* (John 16:33 NKJV). Followers of Christ will have to deal with these issues until He comes back again.

A true leader knows he'll be out front. He knows he'll have his detractors who try and make him stumble. He knows despite seemingly impossible odds, his victory is eternal life in God's presence. Leaders are always on display. In good times and bad they are always on display. Since we're always out front on display it's imperative to live our values. It's imperative to do the right thing. And it's imperative to live a Christ-like life.

PROVIDE READY LEADERS

For this reason I am sending to you Timothy, my son whom I love, who is faithful in the Lord. He will remind you of my way of life in Christ Jesus, which agrees with what I teach everywhere in every church.

1 Corinthians 4:17

Paul sent Timothy to Corinth *for this reason.* Timothy was one of the, if not the greatest protégées of Paul. With Paul's stamp of approval, *faithful in the Lord,* he told the Corinthians how Timothy would remind them *of my way of life in Christ Jesus, which agrees with what I teach everywhere in every church.* In one verse we learn so much.

Timothy had proven himself to Paul. Paul could put Timothy virtually anywhere, and know that Timothy would lead as Paul wanted. Paul knew Timothy knew "*my way of life*" and Paul's way was consistent and Paul's way was commissioned by Christ.

True leaders build other leaders. And these other leaders ensure an organization will continue to succeed in whatever endeavor. A true test of leadership is when a leader can be replaced and there is no loss of productivity. This is a reason I love the military. As people progress in age, experience and rank everyone around them is also progressing in age, experience and rank and the lower ranks are continuing to be refilled. This cycle will continue in perpetuity.

When follow-on leaders and regimes continue to build and do better on the successes of previous leaders and regimes, this proves the value of having ready leaders. Weak minded men won't train their followers to replace them, so when that guy leaves, the organization may suffer.

Christ has had and needs ready leaders. Paul had ready leaders. Leaders are needed regardless of environment. True leaders must provide ready leaders.

IMITATE ME

Therefore I urge you to imitate me.

1 Corinthians 4:16

This is an impassioned plea to the Corinthians. Paul wrote how Christians should live their life and urged the Corinthians to live right. True leaders are secure in their own skin. So a challenge to *imitate me* means do as I do; follow those that follow me (Timothy); use me as the example. Leaders need to be a good example for their organizations.

Ironically, leadership by example works both ways: good and bad. An organization desires its members to follow the good leaders. In some organizations, members may follow the bad leaders. So when Paul said *imitate me,* he knew he was the example to follow.

I've found some men are great at what they do. However, they don't necessarily want to be in charge or be the leader. A true leader wants the responsibility of leadership and wants his followers to imitate him. Michael Jordan, Larry Bird, and Joe Montana wanted the ball in crunch time. That's a leader.

DO NOT AIR YOUR DIRTY LAUNDRY

But instead, one brother goes to law against another—and this in front of unbelievers!

1 Corinthians 6:6

Civil cases could be handled by Jews/Christians and criminal cases were handled by the Roman authorities. It appeared Paul was counseling against those who had taken their case outside the Church to *unbelievers*. Paul argued they may not be as qualified as a believer, even with a believer who was not as adept, assuming that an unbeliever would not rule in a godly way.

More simply: don't air your dirty laundry. An organization's members should be loyal to it, not bring trivial or embarrassing things outside the organization. This isn't to say there is never a time to squelch illegal or unsafe issues, when those issues can be handled through the proper channels.

When you go outside your organization to resolve an issue, or when you discuss issues not meant for those outside your organization this shows a lack of respect, loyalty, and discipline to the organization, as well as a lack of respect and loyalty to the leader.

GET RID OF
THE BAD APPLE

Your boasting is not good. Don't you know that a little yeast works through the whole batch of dough? Get rid of the old yeast that you may be a new batch without yeast—as you really are. For Christ, our Passover lamb, has been sacrificed.

1 Corinthians 5:6-7

True leaders try to salvage every person in their organization. Some believe there are no bad students only bad teachers. However, if a person, despite all normal efforts, refuses to get on board with organizational norms or your plan as the leader, you have to cut him away. You shouldn't so much worry about the people that you don't hire as much as the people you don't fire when firing is necessary.

Here Paul discussed the sexual immorality in Corinth. It appeared this immorality was happening between a man and his father's wife (not his mother). This was a huge sin and just bad morals even now. Yeast or leaven in Scripture normally symbolized sin and here it refers to the prohibition of yeast in the bread during the Passover Feast. Moms then and now continue to use the analogy of "a little yeast…"

Paul told the Corinthians to *get rid of the old yeast*. Organizations, and in this case the Church, need to attain and maintain discipline. Paul instructed them to take care of this issue. As a leader you need to be cognizant of corruption or bad influence, because left unchecked, it may harm a large portion if not your whole organization.

WHEN IN ROME DO AS THE ROMANS DO...WITH ONE EXCEPTION

To those not having the law I became like one not having the law (though I am not free from God's law but am under Christ's law), so as to win those not having the law.

1 Corinthians 9:21

Paul was a Jew and remained a Jew. He didn't give up being a Jew in the name of Christianity. However, he knew that Gentiles didn't need to follow the Law to be saved. He taught and preached that salvation came from belief in Jesus Christ the Son of God. The Law appeared to stifle belief in Christ. The Law appeared to hamper the growth of Jews to become Christians. Paul didn't say the Law didn't matter but, for example, he did say a Gentile being circumcised or uncircumcised did not get him into or keep him out of heaven.

To accommodate the Gentiles Paul didn't push his Jewishness on them. He believed in the law of grace and the law of love: in the context of a personal relationship with Jesus. He knew that attempting to keep all the laws with respect to food and sacrifices did not earn salvation.

When in Rome do as Romans do, is as old as the Roman Empire. There are some that say "go along to get along." I've also heard, "cooperate and graduate." Paul accommodated the Gentiles to win them to Christ but not at the risk of the Law of God or the Law of Christ.

In your organization, in your leadership environments, in your world it is counterproductive to have nothing but "one and done" rules. I used to think there should be more, I realize now there must be some compromise. I do believe that there should be more - but not as much as I originally thought.

A true leader accommodates his people to get the most out of them; to enable initiative; to allow creativity; and to build other leaders. However, there must remain those critical few principles that you, as the leader, will not bend on.

STRIVE FOR THE TRUE PRIZE

No, I beat my body and make it my slave so that after I have preached to others, I myself will not be disqualified for the prize.

1 Corinthians 9:27

Paul used a lot of references to athletics and games in some preceding verses. Here he referred to the prize as salvation but also the prize is the race. Striving for an award or prize after competing in a competition is the wrong objective. Discipline in athletics and sport is a must-have. However, in our race it needs to be toward Christ. Paul demanded discipline in serving Christ.

Most leaders are achievement oriented. If you do not strive for accomplishment, you will not accomplish anything. It sounds obvious. But if you are a leader that does not push the envelope your organization will not achieve anything. True leaders need to keep the true prize as the objective, not the little awards along the way. Individual performance should be recognized but not at the risk of the ultimate goal.

Running the race toward Christ requires discipline. It seems to me that in our comfort-seeking culture, where the motto is "No Pain, No Pain," we have lost the importance of hard work and discipline. Discipline is not always fun, easy, or comfortable. Sometimes it requires us to push through our pain thresholds believing that we will be better persons and more like our Savior on the other side of pain.

The prize is truly the only thing worth striving for. As a leader, strive for the true prize in your environment. It will focus you and enable you not to be hampered by the less important accolades along the way.

UNITY OF THE TEAM

Because there is one loaf, we, who are many, are one body, for we all partake of the one loaf.

1 Corinthians 10:17

Here, Paul was discussing the Lord's Supper. The bread symbolizes the unity of the Church. The one bread of life, of course, is Jesus. The collective worship of Christians symbolizes their unity. The act of partaking in the body and blood of Christ is perhaps one of the most unifying acts a Christian takes with his fellow believers and with our God!

Good organizations are unified. Good organizations have loyal teams of teams. All organizations have some form of teams. Without teams you would not need leaders. A team by definition is united for a common goal. Some teams are better than others. But the best teams, those that are the most successful, those that are the most happy, and those that display the most harmony and productivity are united.

I was privileged to have served on "Silver Team" at a former unit. This team meant everything to me and we truly bonded over the many years I was there. We loved each other, we at times hated each other, we pushed each other, and more importantly we were there for each other no matter what. On one winter training trip in the back mountains of Oregon we experienced a ton of highs, some lows, some tough love, and a lifetime of experiences and laughs. Those that were on that trip will all have the memories. Only true teams can get to that level.

True leaders know the value of united teams. True leaders know how to influence, motivate, and inspire for team accomplishment. Focus on your one or critical few objectives and unite around it/them.

USE YOUR GIFTS FOR THE COMMON GOOD

Now to each one the manifestation of the Spirit is given for the common good.

1 Corinthians 12:7

All believers are given gifts for the common good. The hard part is discovering those gifts and then using them to build His kingdom. My mission is to *Positively Influence Lives*. I do this through my gifts: leading, speaking, and teaching.

Our gifts are meant to glorify God and build His kingdom. Our gifts are not meant for selfish gain. Each one of us must use our gifts as He intended. How do you find your gift if you are not aware of it (or them)? I believe through prayer, reading the Word, meditating on it, and with the help of thoughtful counsel, anyone can find his gifting.

We must be about our Father's business. Now that I know my gifts, I strive to glorify God every day. I look for opportunities for the common good. I volunteer in areas that would be impacted by my gifts.

Use your gifts for the common good. Regardless of environment, leaders lead. Regardless of environment, your gifts are probably needed and can be used; use them for the common good.

SYNERGY

The body is a unit, though it is made up of many parts; and though all its parts are many, they form one body. So it is with Christ.

1 Corinthians 12:12

Each part of the body, even though it may do something unique for the whole body, is dependent upon all the other parts. And this is the same as the Body of Christ. Each of us is unique but together we are of the same accord.

Synergy means the whole is greater than the sum of each individual part. With the human body, the Church, or an organization, all the parts may be diverse but also have unity. We are more powerful together than separate.

A true leader will synergize his organization with the various talents of his people. A true leader will know his mission or objective so well that he'll also know the correct man to undertake it. This reminds me of a quote I've heard, "Who should sing tenor?" "The tenor should sing tenor, of course."

DIVERSITY

But in fact God has arranged the parts in the body, every one of them, just as he wanted them to be.

1 Corinthians 12:18

God has a master plan for all of us. He laid us out as He wanted us to be. He has given us all gifts to accomplish His will. The diversity of our gifts is what makes us strong and unique. Using Paul's *body* analogy, the eye is the eye, not the ear. And the foot has its own responsibility, not that of the hand.

A true leader will understand the value of a diverse group of people. Remember, it's the differences of the parts of the body that make the body. God's grace is for all people. God's plan includes all people. He didn't make us different so that we can all be doing divergent things.

Even though there is diversity with the human body and among people the common goal is still the common goal.

ALL ARE IMPORTANT

On the contrary, those parts of the body that seem to be weaker are indispensable,

1 Corinthians 12:22

Continuing with Paul's analogy of the human body there are some parts perceived to be less important than others, but all are indispensable. Assuming many factors, not least of which is everyone in your organization wants to be there, all parts of your organization are indispensable.

We need to distinguish one's role from one's notoriety. It's easy to think some members are more or less important than others. In a secular world this is done every day. I at times also fall into this trap. A true leader finds a duty or task that each person of his organization can and will accomplish.

God didn't make any member of his Church more or less important than anyone else. Leaders must maximize each member of their organizations regardless of their perceived importance.

ALL FOR ONE AND ONE FOR ALL

If one part suffers, every part suffers with it; if one part is honored, every part rejoices with it.

1 Corinthians 12:26

In the Church, if one suffers there is suffering within the Church. If there is one honored, all should rejoice. This is how it should be. We are commanded to love one another. If we all truly did, this life would be easier. However, it appears because of petty differences, lack of respect, and ultimately a lack of love, there doesn't appear to be as much "all for one and one for all" as there should be.

In very special organizations there is shared pain and shared victory regardless of who it is in reference to. If a leader can get to this harmony in his organization he will achieve the highest of levels.

Leaders should build an environment where all people take personal responsibility and accountability for the team and where no one truly cares who gets the credit for success.

LEADERS ARE ORGANIZED

But everything should be done in a fitting and orderly way.

1 Corinthians 14:40

This is the last verse in 1 Corinthians 14 and follows Paul's instructions and insight about prophesying and orderly worship. Paul wanted the church at Corinth to function in a fitting and orderly way. Organizations should function in a fitting and orderly way.

Leaders are organized. If you watch a good leader, you'll notice that he has certain patterns and processes that make him more effective and efficient. A lot of these patterns and processes are repeatable and enable his followers to also more effectively operate.

No one wants to *not know* what to do on any given day. Leaders who are organized in their personal administration and organizational functioning propel their organizations as opposed to wasting valuable resources dealing with issues they shouldn't have to deal with.

Organize for efficiency, but more importantly, organize for effectiveness.

HUMBLE IN YOUR POSITION

For I am the least of the apostles and do not even deserve to be called an apostle, because I persecuted the church of God.

1 Corinthians 15:9

Paul knew how horrid his past was. He knew how terribly he treated believers. That's what makes his conversion and his ministry so awesome. In verse 10 we see *by the grace of God I am what I am, and his grace to me was not without effect. No, I worked harder than all of them—yet not I, but the grace of God that was with me.* If you truly understand what Paul did, you'd realize how truly impossible his mission was; yet he was extremely humble and gave all the credit to God.

Humility is sometimes viewed as weakness. However, Paul, like Jesus, was humble in everything he did. To be a true servant leader mandates humility. A leader is responsible for his people. People can easily see through the nonsense and pomp, but a truly humble leader gets the most out of his people.

I love "I worked harder than all of them." I wrote the book on "working smarter not harder" but once in a while, plain old hard work is what makes organizations and leaders a success. But, along the way, a leader must be humble. He cannot and must not take credit for successes or publicize his successes. Humility requires a laser focus on other people and off self.

Be humble in your position.

DON'T BE MISLED BY BAD DOCTRINE

Do not be misled: 'Bad company corrupts good character.'

1 Corinthians 15:33

In 1 Corinthians 15 Paul gave a great dissertation on the Resurrection of Jesus and through facts and logic proved the gospel. In verse 32 Paul quoted the Greek poet Meander; someone the Corinthians would know (know your audience). Paul reminded the Corinthians that they were being taught there was no resurrection by *bad company*. This was bad doctrine. And the *bad company* was *corrupting* the *good character* of those who hold to the correct doctrine.

Paul's First Letter to the Corinthians is probably one of his more pointed and corrective letters he wrote. There were bad seeds in Corinth. There were bad people in Corinth. Paul wanted to ensure he reiterated the gospel and proper living. Throughout the letter he gave very constructive guidance and commands.

In 15:33 Paul again focused on an area that mandated true leadership: maintaining proper doctrine. Throughout time new and different leadership styles have come and gone. Some were more dictatorial, others were more laissez faire. You can see when a sports team fires a coach who say, for example, was a "player's coach." They'll turn around and bring in the "disciplinarian." And vice versa, some may fire the disciplinarian and bring in the more empathetic guy.

Regardless of the style, true leaders do not budge on doctrine… the gospel.

YOUR WORK IS NOT IN VAIN

Therefore, my dear brothers, stand firm. Let nothing move you. Always give yourselves fully to the work of the Lord, because you know that your labor in the Lord is not in vain.

1 Corinthians 15:58

This is the last verse in 1 Corinthians 15 and completes some great Pauline instruction. *Therefore,* as a former pastor has always said, was "there for" a reason; pointing back to everything Paul just said; probably specifically chapter 15; Jesus' resurrection.

Serving Jesus is not in vain. Serving Jesus is not useless. God will reward us in heaven for our works on earth. This is Scripture and is irrefutable. God's desire for us is to Glorify Him. Those that do will be rewarded.

Despite the seemingly impossible odds, your work is not in vain. There are times when it seems your work is all for naught; don't believe it. If your mission is right then your work will pay off. It's human nature to doubt when things are tough or unfair or seem unpopular.

A true leader keeps his people focused on the mission, on correct doctrine, on the core values, on the work and knows each individual's work is not in vain.

BE STRONG IN YOUR FAITH

Be on your guard; stand firm in the faith; be men of courage; be strong.
1 Corinthians 16:13

Here Paul concluded this letter to the Corinthians. It's one verse that encapsulates so much teaching; *be on your guard;* be diligent in carrying out the will of God; *stand firm in the faith;* another timely reminder; *be men of courage* and *be strong.* This is a mark of maturity and a caution against being swept away like a child.

Paul was nothing if not consistent. Paul was nothing if not persistent. True leaders emulate this verse. A true leader's followers need to emulate this verse. Paul's consistency and persistency are his hallmarks.

Men are capable of doing amazing things, and often times seemingly impossible things, given the right circumstances. In my experience, because my men had been on their guard, stood firm, were courageous and strong, they exceeded any worldly standard.

Your people can do virtually anything with faith. Faith comes from knowing the grace of God. It can also come from the confidence a leader has in his people. Paul reminded the Corinthians of some simple actions that would serve them well.

LEADERS HAVE COMPASSION

Praise be to the God and Father of our Lord Jesus Christ, the Father of compassion and the God of all comfort, who comforts us in all our troubles, so that we can comfort those in any trouble with the comfort we ourselves have received from God.

2 Corinthians 1:3-4

Here Paul has written at least his second letter to the Corinthians. He reminds the Corinthians true comfort only comes from God Himself. He also used three descriptions for God: *Father of our Lord Jesus Christ; Father of compassion;* and *God of all comfort.*

With the compassion only found in God we can also comfort others in trouble. A leader needs to have and exude compassion. Our people need to know we care about them, and will be there when needed. Nothing can compare to God's love and compassion. A true leader knows his people are the ones that accomplish the mission. A true leader will be there no matter where, no matter when, no matter what.

RUMOR CONTROL

When I planned this, did I do it lightly? Or do I make my plans in a worldly manner so that in the same breath I say, "Yes, yes" and "No, no"?

2 Corinthians 1:17

In this letter to the Corinthians, Paul had written yet another correction of potential lies or false teaching. His two rhetorical questions point to either a response to a letter, or to a verbal rumor in circulation that he was not coming as originally planned (1 Cor. 16:5-7).

Perhaps it was in response to those telling the believing Corinthians that Paul could not be trusted or relied upon. Regardless, Paul was setting it straight, by being straight. Don't mince words.

If rumors are running amuck, square them away. It's better to set the story straight, than let rumors or innuendos go unchallenged. I'm reminded of the movie *Aliens 3*, when they're on that 'prison' planet and the warden comes to a gathering of the prison population stating "Rumor Control….here are the facts!" He still gets whacked, but he wanted to ensure his men (a precarious bunch to say the least) did not have bad information, and consequently do regrettable things based on the bad info.

DO NOT LOSE HEART

Therefore we do not lose heart. Though outwardly we are wasting away, yet inwardly we are being renewed day by day.
                                                            2 Corinthians 4:16

    This world can be hard. This world at times is evil and full of hate, anger, and sin. Paul reminded the Corinthians that despite all he had been through and what they were going through, to not lose heart. Paul reminded them that God raised Jesus from the dead and will raise all of us to be in His presence when that time comes.

    Scripture is full of great examples of how we are to be joyous in Christ. If we allow this world to get us down, we are no good to anyone. However, if through our anguish and despair, we maintain our focus on Jesus, then our reward will be there in Heaven. Paul reminded them that as we grow weaker physically, we should also be growing stronger spiritually.

    You can only be *renewed* with Jesus. True leaders have to have Jesus in their hearts. And when they go through hard times, and they all do; their joyousness during those times will be contagious.

TO LIVE ON

known, yet regarded as unknown; dying, and yet we live on; beaten, and yet not killed;"

2 Corinthians 6:9

Here Paul discussed his hardships. It's hard to imagine what Paul physically went through in his day; and that's just what is in Scripture. Paul reminded the Corinthians that despite all of his hardships he had turned all the negatives into positives (verses 4-10).

He was a great example for the Corinthians and expected the same from them. Paul's hardships are articulated throughout Acts and his 13 letters. Paul appeared to have persevered more than anyone else given the same circumstances.

True leaders will be that example for others to follow. Those leaders I most admired never slacked off. They never took it easy. They never cut corners. And oftentimes did more than their people and definitely more than they had to. Those are the men that are successful.

True leaders may have to put up with a figurative or maybe even a literal beating, but as long as it does not kill them, they can press on with their mission and be that example for their organizations.

DO NOT BE YOKED TOGETHER WITH UNBELIEVERS

Do not be yoked together with unbelievers. For what do righteousness and wickedness have in common? Or what fellowship can light have with darkness?

2 Corinthians 6:14

Christians are to love everyone and witness to everyone. We are to try and make disciples regardless of environment. However, here in verse 14 and in other parts of scripture it's clear believers are not supposed to consort with unbelievers.

We are to try and minister to them, but we are not to agree with or condone their actions, their teachings, or their beliefs. Paul rhetorically asked the Corinthians about the harmony between the two groups. What did they have in common? What agreements did they have?

A true leader of an organization must put the right people in the right jobs. Notice I didn't say the best people; I mean the right people. Despite all of your efforts, you may be unable to get enough, or anything, out of some people. I only use an analogy of *unbeliever* in this respect. If a person simply does not respond to you, you are not to be yoked with him.

I knew of a pastor that preached on this topic once yet he rented some property to a non-believer and the pastor knew he was a non-believer. He apparently tried to justify this by saying "I am witnessing to him." As far as I know, he is still renting to him. Marriage, close personal relationships, business partnerships are what *yoked* means. Scripture says we're not to be *yoked* to *unbelievers*.

TOUGH LOVE

Godly sorrow brings repentance that leads to salvation and leaves no regret, but worldly sorrow brings death.

2 Corinthians 7:10

Read verses eight and nine. Paul said he was not sorry for what he said in a previous letter, because it led them to repentance. Even though his guidance may have appeared tough on some folks, his guidance was truth. Never be afraid to espouse and demand truth. This sounds cliché, but at the end of the day truth is always the best way to go.

True leaders may have to show tough love. In your heart you love your people, but tough love means you make a tough call in love, because you know it will be the better course of action for people. What separates the great leaders is they do it without being antagonistic or sarcastic.

Without giving away specifics, I personally experienced this. Ken Rodriguez was my Commander, Director of Operations and Team Leader during portions of our careers. I had a personal issue that the unit mission was potentially going to infringe upon. I addressed it with him and he gave me tough love.

Suffice to say he was right, it all panned out, and I learned from it. As important as learning from it was, he did it in a manner that I had no ill will toward him afterwards, nor was I demoralized at all. True leaders need to show tough love when need be.

BE A CHEERFUL GIVER

Each man should give what he has decided in his heart to give, not reluctantly or under compulsion, for God loves a cheerful giver.

2 Corinthians 9:7

My family and I were on vacation to Myrtle Beach one time, and my former boss allowed us to use his place. He has a phenomenal house; it is first class with a bunch of great amenities. He freely let us enjoy it. As we were driving to dinner one night, I don't remember what the subject was, but I commented to my wife Tammie how special it was, when someone has the means and freely gives it away. Mr. DiSantis is like that. He has the means, and cheerfully gives.

Also during that vacation it was around the time the New York Yankees owner George Steinbrenner had passed away. During the week following his death a lot of reporting about Mr. Steinbrenner's philanthropy came to light. Wow, very few people, especially me, knew of all his charity and giving over the years. There was a perception of his "tough" and "win at all costs" demeanor, but what most people didn't know is that he used his wealth to help make people's lives better.

When you give to charity, or give to your church, or give to your employees, or do something for someone else, doing it without a lot of fanfare is special. It's not really special when you make a big pronouncement or attempt to get a lot of headlines.

God loves a cheerful giver. Everything we have is from Him. We should give it away. Be a cheerful giver.

BE A SOWER

Remember this: Whoever sows sparingly will also reap sparingly, and whoever sows generously will also reap generously.

2 Corinthians 9:6

Paul is trying to collect the offering for the church in Jerusalem. This appears to be an oft-used message in churches ad infinitum. *Whoever sows sparingly will also reap sparingly, and whoever sows generously will also reap generously.* This also implies other opportunities to sow with your people.

Think about the opportunities leaders have with sowing generously and vice versa. Every single time you have interaction with someone, you are sowing. One of my best friends Mike Lamonica is a phenomenal sower. He is generous with his money and he is phenomenally generous with his time. I've watched literally over 25+ years how he sows with virtually every person he comes in contact with. He either shares a kind word, a teaching point, or a moment of encouragement. And you can see the recipient is better for it at that time and over the long term. Remember, without other people and a task to be done, leaders are not necessary. So in every single environment you are with people, you will have an opportunity to sow.

A positive word, encouragement, pat on the back, praise, an answer to a question, are all examples of sowing generously. Also investing in your people with additional training, experiences, and skills is sowing generously. Developing your people is also positively sowing.

True leaders are master sowers. They do it generously and they do it deep and wide across their organizations. Be a sower.

BOAST IN THE LORD

For even if I boast somewhat freely about the authority the Lord gave us for building you up rather than pulling you down, I will not be ashamed of it.

2 Corinthians 10:8

Paul was in a pretty powerful position. He was ordained by Christ, called by God, to deliver the gospel to the Gentiles. This is irrefutable. Paul talked about countless examples of his readers' boasting. Paul's boasting was in the Lord.

True leaders never boast, except about their people. True leaders are humble in Christ and lead by example. Boasting takes the focus off of Christ or off your people, and puts it on you, which is where it should not be. Boasting also proves you are not humble.

Leaders have tremendous authority, and also tremendous responsibility. True leaders use this authority for *building up,* not *pulling down.* Leaders should never be ashamed of doing their duty.

ALWAYS BE AUTHENTIC

Such people should realize that what we are in our letters when we are absent, we will be in our actions when we are present.

2 Corinthians 10:11

In 10:10 Paul intimates that the Corinthians thought Paul to be different in his letters than in person. They also appeared to say that Paul was *unimpressive* in person. On the contrary, Paul was authentic in every environment. And I would guess he was very impressive in his message. Remember, some leaders are known for the content of their character, not the size of their shoulders. Paul was that guy.

In my study of the Word, Paul was the master at situational leadership. He gave what people needed, when they needed it, and in the manner they needed it. Obviously Paul's message ruffled some feathers and even caused some to want to kill Paul. Did he ever give up? Never!

True leaders are authentic: true to their mission. My folks knew what they were getting every day. They had no doubt whether in person, on the phone, on weekends, or in some other environment. You should be viewed as authentic, regardless of the environment you're in.

WHAT YOU NEED TO BE A GOOD PUBLIC SPEAKER

I may not be a trained speaker, but I do have knowledge. We have made this perfectly clear to you in every way.

2 Corinthians 11:6

Paul alluded to 11:5 when he talked about the *super-apostles*. Was he comparing his ability to theirs? I don't know if he's being humble or responding to criticism he had received from the Corinthians about his supposed lack of public speaking ability. I think Paul was a phenomenal public speaker. How else would he have so masterfully delivered the gospel to so many who ultimately became believers?

I've always taught there are two major requirements to be a good public speaker. One is you have to have a mastery of your subject. Sure, I've seen some skilled speakers wing their presentation and admittedly were not experts at the subject, but those are rare. If I am speaking to an audience about flux-capacitor maintenance, it's obvious I should be an expert on the subject, or why else am I in front of the audience?

The second requirement is you have to have the physical speaking skills. These include but aren't limited to presence, ability to think on your feet, mastery of language, mastery of context, and the ability to articulate complex subjects in a manner your audience understands.

I believe Paul had both. He obviously was an expert on his subject matter, the gospel. And I would argue he was the master at presentation.

Look through Acts and read all the times he spoke (that Luke recorded) and you'll see he definitely knew his audience, never had stage fright, and spoke in a manner necessary for his particular audience.

Mastery of your subject and physical presentation skills are necessary to become a good public speaker. True leaders, regardless of environment, can speak to any audience, on most any topic and inspire for action.

KEEP ON DOING WHAT I'M DOING

And I will keep on doing what I am doing in order to cut the ground from under those who want an opportunity to be considered equal with us in the things they boast about.

2 Corinthians 11:12

Despite constant obstacles Paul never gave up. I wonder if he ever got down, I assume he did. You need leaders when there is chaos. You need leaders to drive for change. You need leaders when the mission is seemingly impossible. Paul dealt with all that, and kept on doing what he was doing.

True leaders never give up. Imagine in history if all the great leaders didn't press through all the obstacles they had to deal with. We'd live in a more horrible place, I would imagine. Keep on keeping on, is what true leaders do.

If you don't, then your followers can't get to where they need to be. We don't want to follow leaders that don't stay focused on the mission, or change their mind every time they are faced with a challenge.

True leaders keep on doing what they know is right and expect their followers to do the same.

SUFFERING FOR MISSION COMPLETION

Are they servants of Christ? (I am out of my mind to talk like this.) I am more. I have worked much harder, been in prison more frequently, been flogged more severely, and been exposed to death again and again.

2 Corinthians 11:23

Paul described his sufferings in Christ in this section of 2 Corinthians. He also used the diatribe. There was no doubt Paul suffered. Luke quotes Paul and Barnabas in Acts 14:22 about having to go through many hardships to enter the Kingdom of God. Paul did not boast in a conceited way. Paul maintained the most humble nature I believe anyone could have in his situation. And he did all this to accomplish his ultimate mission.

Suffice to say most of us won't have to deal with floggings, shipwrecks, beatings, imprisonment, etc. but we will go through our own type of suffering in the accomplishment of our mission and more importantly in our walk. True leaders stay focused on their mission and let the suffering motivate them to be an example for others, or they use it to validate their progress.

SHOWING GENUINE CONCERN FOR YOUR PEOPLE

Besides everything else, I face daily the pressure of my concern for all the churches.

2 Corinthians 11:28

This follows some phenomenal verses about Paul's sufferings for the cause. Yet through his suffering he continued to show his concern for the Corinthians. He anguished over them and all his people. He yearned for them to believe and live the Christian life. He felt their pain when they struggled. Paul encouraged those who followed him, when a lesser leader may have given up.

John Maxwell said, "People don't care how much you know, until they know how much you care." What a phenomenally true statement. Paul took the gospel, struggling to survive during this period, and forged through impossible obstacles. And to achieve his mission he never stopped caring for his people.

True leaders care about their people. They show their genuineness in everything they do. Paul never complained about his sufferings. He did pray for relief at times, but he never complained. And his demeanor through his sufferings is an example for all of us to emulate. Knowing our leaders care for us makes it easier to also endure.

GOD GIVEN AUTHORITY IS MEANT TO BUILD UP

This is why I write these things when I am absent, that when I come I may not have to be harsh in my use of authority—the authority the Lord gave me for building you up, not for tearing you down.

2 Corinthians 13:10

George H W Bush in his inaugural address said a prayer. He said it was his first act as President. In that prayer he also said, "There is but one just use of power, and it is to serve people." President Bush knew all authority is God-given and we are to use that authority to serve. Paul practiced this about nineteen hundred years earlier.

Why are people confident? Why are some kids happier than others? Why do some people have higher self-esteem than others? I would say partly because in those situations they were built up consistently and persistently. Consequently the opposite is true. Tearing people down not only destroys individuals, it is the quickest way to fail as a leader.

True leaders use their God-given authority to build people up. Build your folks up and your organization's potential could be limitless.

A LEADER AMONGST LEADERS

As for those who seemed to be important—whatever they were makes no difference to me; God does not judge by external appearance—those men added nothing to my message. On the contrary, they saw that I had been entrusted with the task of preaching the gospel to the Gentiles, just as Peter had been to the Jews. For God, who was at work in the ministry of Peter as an apostle to the Jews, was also at work in my ministry as an apostle to the Gentiles.

Galatians 2:6-8

Galatians is one of Paul's letters often used for the biographical information about Paul that we all crave. As many readers of the Bible know, there are gaps in Acts. Galatians fills in some of them. Paul reminded his readers in Galatians 2 that he went to Jerusalem with Barnabas and Titus. Paul not only had naysayers that were believers, but he talked about false brothers infiltrating the church.

In 2:6 It could be easy to say Paul had a rift with those *who seemed to be important*. I believe the lesson is if you know you're right, if you know your mission is important, if you know your objective is to build others up, it should not matter what other leaders say. Paul implies in 2:7-8 that, in essence, each leader is responsible for "his mission" and reminded them they were God ordained.

There have been times in my 27+ years in leadership environments some leaders tried to "one up" others. This does not build others up; it has a negative impact, and definitely does not glorify God. Healthy competition is fine, but positional leaders who attempt to negatively impact other leaders to the detriment of the same organization have issues that need to be fixed.

True leaders are not swayed by what others say or do if they "know" they're right. And true leaders don't allow other leaders to negatively impact their organization.

SAYING NO WHEN ALL AROUND YOU ARE SAYING YES

When Peter came to Antioch, I opposed him to his face, because he was clearly in the wrong.

Galatians 2:11

Not to oversimplify, Paul (after his conversion) knew the coming of the Messiah was for the Jew and the Gentile. Everyone who believes is saved, God shows no favoritism (Romans 2:11). Some Jews thought to be saved you had to become a Jew and live according to the Law. After all, Christianity started with the Jews. Peter's epiphany in Acts 10 showed him God shows no favoritism (Acts 10:34-35). Also check out Acts 15:6-11. However, it appears from this point (Acts 10) until sometime later, Peter still was prejudiced toward Gentiles. So in this verse, Paul commented on a time Peter showed divisiveness, and Paul called him on it.

Remember Abraham was saved *before* circumcision and *before* God gave Moses the Ten Commandments. Abraham was saved because he believed (Romans 4:3), not because of the Law and not because he was a Jew (Romans 4).

I was privileged to be a Chief Master Sergeant in the USAF. When I got promoted I received a nice plaque with the *Chief's Creed* on it. One of the axioms says "able to say no, when all around you are saying yes." True leaders stand up for what is right. True leaders ensure that, even when other popular leaders are in the wrong, there will be correction given, even if at the time it would seem to be going against the grain.

THE COMMON DENOMINATORS

You are all sons of God through faith in Christ Jesus, for all of you who were baptized into Christ have clothed yourselves with Christ. There is neither Jew nor Greek, slave nor free, male nor female, for you are all one in Christ Jesus.

Galatians 3:26-28

A great thing about Christianity is its simplicity of entering: faith in Jesus. Another great thing about Christianity is its inclusiveness. I admit at times I only wanted to be around those that were "like me." This goes against everything Jesus stood for. I fail every day at measuring up, but thank God He's not looking for perfection, He'll take care of that later.

I used to get bent out of shape when some people weren't "exactly" as I wished they were. Through maturity, I realized I simply needed those people to know their role and do their role. Jim Collins says it better in *Good to Great* with "getting the right person in the right seat on the bus." I need to find those one or two common denominators that motivate a person to help our organization accomplish its mission. Some inarguable denominators are integrity, desire (for something), and motivation.

Leaders in most organizations will have a huge diversity of the following: intelligence, culture, race, age, education, motivations, gender, etc. True leaders bring all this together for the common good. You need to find the common denominators. For Christians it's Jesus. Use your organization's common denominators to propel it.

BLUF

The entire law is summed up in a single command: "Love your neighbor as yourself."

Galatians 5:14

This is a phenomenally insightful verse with an amazingly simple command. In the military they often use the acronym "BLUF" which stands for Bottom Line up Front. When you communicate to senior leaders and/or decision makers you want them to know from the first word what you need them to know. So you literally write BLUF in the top of your e-mail or other communication medium, then what you want them to know, otherwise known as the "bottom line."

Don't spend three pages or even three paragraphs "getting" to your point, put your point first, and then add amplifying information. If I can tell you in one sentence what I need from you (by way of action or decision) then I do that. I only add additional information if I have to because it is needed. The BLUF in one sentence says what this communication is all about and nothing else.

You don't necessarily have to actually write BLUF but get to your point right from the start. This will garner understanding early and also focus your audience to what you need early. Paul mastered the BLUF in this one verse. True leaders should use it when necessary.

WHAT IS YOUR MISSION?

In him we were also chosen, having been predestined according to the plan of him who works out everything in conformity with the purpose of his will,

Ephesians 1:11

Being one of His "chosen ones" brings with it great joy and incredible privilege. It also brings great responsibility and requires incredible humility. If you read on, in this same letter by Paul to the Ephesians, in chapter 2, verse 10, Paul says*, "For we are God's workmanship, created in Christ Jesus to do good works, which God prepared in advance for us to do."*

My mission is to Positively Influence Lives. This mission was explained earlier. We were created to fulfill God's mission that He has for us. What is that mission? Some people know it and execute it early in life and everyday thereafter. Others spend a lifetime trying to figure out what their purpose is in life. And still others don't even try to find it.

We were all put here for a reason. It's pretty humbling knowing God has a plan for us and that plan was determined before we were born. Some missions for people include to give, pray, lead, mission, pastor, feed, and many others. Find what it is for you.

We all have gifts and we all have a purpose. A lot of those include exerting some level of leadership. What is your mission? Find it and work on it.

THE FOUNDATION OF AN ORGANIZATION

built on the foundation of the apostles and prophets, with Christ Jesus himself as the chief cornerstone.

Ephesians 2:20

Strong and successful organizations are built on a strong foundation. The foundation is its leaders, and includes THE leader. All members of an organization are at some obvious level. You know who your direct supervisor is and probably who his supervisor is and obviously those who directly report to you. There is a logical hierarchy in most organizations. Strong and successful organizations have great leaders at all levels especially the top.

If Christ is not your cornerstone or is not the cornerstone of your leaders, you or your organization will not be very successful. And if you think you are currently successful without Christ as the cornerstone, you won't be ultimately, or for a long period of time.

In 2:19 Paul reminded the Ephesians they are no longer foreigners and aliens. Their foundation now is the apostles and prophets and Christ as the chief cornerstone. Strong leaders in strong organizations ensure all their people are on the same page. Of course there are nuances in different departments and quirks with different folks, but the foundation is all the same in these organizations.

True leaders build on a strong foundation. Christ needs to be your cornerstone.

COMMANDER'S INTENT

His intent was that now, through the church, the manifold wisdom of God should be made known to the rulers and authorities in the heavenly realms,

Ephesians 3:10

Ephesians is a great letter. So much is said in only six chapters. Paul is discussing that *now* (3:5) God's intent has been made known. Ephesians deserves consistent study.

My lesson in this verse is Commander's Intent. In the military, when an organization was given a mission, they were also provided their commander's intent - for not only the next level commander, but also the second level up. Commander's intent, in a statement, tells the organization who received the mission what the expectation is.

There are different schools of thought on how to best provide commander's intent to the lower level organizations but in essence it includes: purpose, method and endstate. Once you've read it, you normally have no doubt what your commander wants.

When you receive a mission, make sure you know your commander's (boss') intent. When you give a mission, make sure you provide your intent.

LIVE A WORTHY LIFE

As a prisoner for the Lord, then, I urge you to live a life worthy of the calling you have received.

Ephesians 4:1

Christians are not better than nonbelievers, just better off. We are blessed to be in the body of Christ. Those who have been called should celebrate and live worthy lives daily. Those who are called should be good examples of their calling.

I've often heard that the dash on your headstone is your life and what you accomplished. What will your dash say? Oftentimes I just want Meaghan and Sophia to know me as the greatest Dad on the planet, and everything else will take care of itself. Other times, I just want Tammie to know I'm the best husband I can be. But obviously there are other things in our life, not as important however, but environments we all find ourselves in.

The most obvious is our career. Leaders must live a worthy life. True leaders are great examples in word, deed, and faith. I can't count how many times a supposed leader had put out guidance "do this" or "don't do that" or "because I said so" and it fell on deaf ears because he was not worthy to follow. I was stationed with a guy that outranked me. He had a reputation of a loud mouth and a tough guy. It got to be an ongoing joke. He used to constantly rip into people about various things. And then he failed his PT test. Almost instantly his loud mouth went ignored.

To be worthy you must first and foremost be trusted. Paul reminded us in 4:2 to *be completely humble and gentle; be patient, bearing with one another in love.* True leaders live a worthy life. Everything about them is to be modeled or emulated.

SOME ARE DESTINED TO BE LEADERS

to prepare God's people for works of service, so that the body of Christ may be built up

Ephesians 4:12

Verse 11 shows that God "gave" some to be apostles, or prophets, or evangelists, or pastors, or teachers and into verse 12 *to prepare God's people*. Leaders lead. Earlier I discussed that leaders are born and made, even though a lot of folks don't ascribe to the born part. This is another of many verses proving that God destines some people to be leaders.

True leaders prepare their people. Verse 12 is so simple and yet says so much: *to prepare God's people for works of service, so that the body of Christ may be built up*. Action: to prepare. From whom: God. To whom: people. What: works of service. Why: so that the body of Christ may be built up. Your works of service may be digging ditches, running a bank, or leading a country. Leadership can be defined as a person, in any environment, influencing people, who are striving to achieve a goal.

I would argue not every single person in a leadership position is "destined" to be there. However, I take serious where I'm at now and where I've been. For me, it was no accident. For others, it is no accident. Leaders lead and in a lot of occasions are destined to be there. And true leaders ensure their works of service build others up.

THE WHOLE BODY

From him the whole body, joined and held together by every supporting ligament, grows and builds itself up in love, as each part does its work.
Ephesians 4:16

Synergy means the sum of the whole is greater than its individual parts. This verse completes a section about the unity in the body of Christ. The *whole body* is the church. The church is made up of all believers. Every single person has value and is important to the whole. Together everyone achieves more (TEAM). That is synergy.

Organizations are made up of diverse individuals. In some organizations, the members are a lot alike, but those organizations are unique. A leader's desire is that his whole organization works together toward a common goal. If everyone works together, only then can an organization achieve its potential.

Each part must do its work. Cherish those organizations where every single member has bought into the vision, is trained and equipped to fulfill their mission, and have the core values to operate at maximum effectiveness. True leaders synergize for maximum effectiveness.

LEAD BY BUILDING UP

> *Do not let any unwholesome talk come out of your mouths, but only what is helpful for building others up according to their needs, that it may benefit those who listen.*
>
> Ephesians 4:29

I am not proud of it but admittedly I have had *unwholesome talk* a lot in my life, especially in my 20-30s. I have matured and sometimes it is still prevalent. The only words that should come out of your mouth "should" be words that build others up. I know that and you know that.

I aspire that every word I use around people builds them up, edifies them, or is otherwise construed as positive. I've been in environments, and have deserved a tongue lashing. I have deserved some unwholesome talk. And I would argue that in those times the person delivering it, was either holding me accountable, was truly disappointed in me, or thought that was the method to motivate for action.

I have held and will continue to hold the people I supervise accountable. However, I need to also hold myself accountable to ensure I'm always building them up. Studies have proven folks with high self esteem, amongst other things, were raised in a positive uplifting environment. People who are constantly encouraged are more often than not going to achieve their potential. Lead by building others up.

STRIVE TO LIVE WISELY; WITH WISDOM

Be very careful, then, how you live—not as unwise but as wise,

Ephesians 5:15

This almost sounds like one of King Solomon's proverbs. Paul encouraged the Ephesians to live wisely. He planted this church. He taught the gospel to them. He encouraged them to continue in the faith with what they knew and with what he taught. I think he toiled with the Ephesians wanting to hear "well done my good and faithful servant."

This is sound advice. In a lot of the Leadership seminars I teach I normally end my session by reminding my audience, normally Special Operations studs that have their whole life ahead of them, to use good judgment. This judgment only comes from being wise.

Wisdom also comes with age. However, as you experience wisdom, regardless if you're young or old you should continue to try and build upon it. Most people don't want to do stupid things. Most people don't want to screw up. Most people want to do well. Because of circumstance, environment, and especially choices, people are where they are because of the choices they've made. Live wisely. Wise leaders lead by example.

TRAINING AND INSTRUCTION

Fathers, do not exasperate your children; instead, bring them up in the training and instruction of the Lord.

Ephesians 6:4

Paul cautions not to "exasperate" your children, or provoke them to anger. The world needs discipline. Organizations need discipline. When Paul is talking about *training and instruction* not only is he talking about the obvious, but also the discipline that goes along with it.

Leaders teach their folks or get them the instruction they need for them to perform what the organization needs them to do. Leaders also need to provide discipline to their folks. Sometimes the word discipline conjures up the image of spanking a child, or whipping a prisoner, or doing something physical to someone in a negative way. This is not the case in this context.

Most followers I've been associated with actually want the discipline. They actually want the training and instruction that goes with achieving their highest potential. They want to operate in a high expectation environment. They actually operate better when the expectations are high. *Training and instructing* our folks to do what we need them to do is a necessity, not a luxury, not merely a nice thing to have.

True leaders ensure their members are properly trained and able to operate within a disciplined environment that enables success.

GOOD WORK WILL GET REWARDED

because you know that the Lord will reward everyone for whatever good he does, whether he is slave or free.

Ephesians 6:8

This follows three verses where Paul commands *slaves to obey*. Read these four verses, they are very insightful. The Lord is the One True God. He will reward all *good* regardless of your status while on this Earth.

One of my purposes for writing this book was to glorify God. You glorify God by doing good. Not because it will "earn" your salvation. Not because you're trying to earn points. Not because you have to because someone is keeping score. You glorify God because you want to out of love and so "others see thee in us" as a former deacon would say.

True leaders do good for their folks not because of accolades they hope to receive or because it will make them appear cool, but because that is what true leaders do.

EQUIP YOUR TEAM

Finally, be strong in the Lord and in his mighty power. Put on the full armor of God so that you can take your stand against the devil's schemes.
Ephesians 6:10-11

Paul reminded believers to protect themselves from Satan by putting on the full armor of God. There is no better protection than that. In a sense Paul was equipping his followers.

A leader needs to provide resources to his teammates to accomplish whatever mission they have. An under-resourced team will underperform. Resources include time, material, funding, training, manpower and a myriad of others.

Teams cannot do their jobs unless they've been properly equipped with what they need. A critical resource to equip your team with is training. A lot of times, there appeared to be an ability to get enough money (not all but enough); enough time; enough manpower, but a leader cannot overemphasize training.

Properly equip your team and get them the training to make them as effective as possible.

DECLARE IT FEARLESSLY

for which I am an ambassador in chains. Pray that I may declare it fearlessly, as I should.

Ephesians 6:20

Following the section on the *Armor of God*, Paul asked for prayer. He asked his brothers to pray that he would be able to declare the gospel fearlessly. Imagine if you could declare truth without fear. Think about it. How many times haven't you done something that you knew you should have but didn't out of fear? That fear can take many forms including: ridicule, being fired, being punished, your friends may think less of you, and many other scenarios.

Paul wanted to be able to *declare it fearlessly*. He asked for this prayer whenever he opened his mouth. The Spirit is with believers. We are promised that He will speak for us. We only need to trust in Him.

True leaders are fearless. I didn't say reckless. I didn't say careless. I said fearless. They know their mission, they know the steps it takes to achieve the mission and they fearlessly take strides toward that mission accomplishment.

Pray that you can fearlessly achieve God's mission for your life.

LEAD FROM THE FRONT

Because of my chains, most of the brothers in the Lord have been encouraged to speak the word of God more courageously and fearlessly.
Philippians 1:14

Paul wrote this letter from prison. He discussed how his circumstances encouraged other brothers to advance the gospel. Paul was in prison! And he used the time to offer encouragement. He used this time to lead from the front. In the military, one of the most definitive examples of leading from the front that we had, was when the leader(s) did what the sled dogs did. Paul was in prison! And despite this he was still preaching and teaching.

Some leaders had no credibility because they were "do as I say not as I do" leaders. This is not to say that all leaders all the time need to do the grunt work, however it means the leader "gets his hands dirty" when he has to. How encouraging is it when you see your leader right next to you doing what he's asking you to do? From experience, I can tell you it's priceless.

Paul led from the front and paid the ultimate sacrifice. Paul knew he would go wherever God needed him to go. He wrote about his trials and tribulations on numerous occasions. He knew he would be treated with prejudice by not only Gentiles but also Jews. He knew he would die for Christ. And yet he led from the front.

True leaders lead by action. True leaders provide encouragement by doing what they expect their followers to do. True leaders will always do more than they expect from their followers and will always lead from the front.

LEADERS ARE HUMBLE

Do nothing out of selfish ambition or vain conceit, but in humility consider others better than yourselves.

Philippians 2:3

Being humble or showing humility is one of the hardest things for me to do. It's cliché to say I've come a long way (I have) but I have tons more to improve. Leaders are humble. They always think of others over themselves.

Imagine if, across every organization, there were leaders that were only concerned with the benefit of others over themselves. What if there were leaders who did not exhibit *selfish ambition or vain conceit?* The organizations would be a lot more successful. They would be a lot more Christ-like. Their organizations would be a lot better places to work.

Leaders are servants. Christ is the greatest example of a humble servant. He willingly died for all humanity's sins. Verse 3 precedes some phenomenal poetry by Paul in verses 4-11 when he asked us all to imitate Christ's humility.

True leaders are humble. They do not seek personal gain. They do not seek public praise. They put others first. Their ambition is based on the common good. Live a humble life.

PRAISE IN PUBLIC

I have no one else like him, who takes a genuine interest in your welfare.
Philippians 2:20

The old adage is "praise in public and scold in private." Paul was the master of praising in public. Paul loved Timothy. Timothy stuck by Paul. Timothy became the man he did because of Paul. Here Paul told the Philippians he had *no one else like him*. That's high praise. Think about that. Paul was in prison, he had traveled thousands of miles planting churches, raised numerous leaders, spread the gospel and over those many years, Timothy and only Timothy got this public praise.

This verse could inspire many other lessons. You cannot imagine the value that praising in public has on your folks. From experience it's worth more than most things. First, the praise has to actually be warranted. A leader will lose credibility for praising folks for doing things they are supposed to do. Leaders should "catch people doing things right." (Maxwell) Then tell everyone about it.

Praising in public does many things. It gives credit where credit is due. It shows your appreciation for the receiver. It shows humility on the one doing the praising. It tells the whole organization something good about one of their own. It tells the whole organization what the leader finds praise worthy. And lets everyone know they can expect the same thing in similar situations.

True leaders praise their folks in public.

SOME THINGS JUST DON'T MATTER

If anyone else thinks he has reasons to put confidence in the flesh, I have more: circumcised on the eighth day, of the people of Israel, of the tribe of Benjamin, a Hebrew of Hebrews; in regard to the law, a Pharisee; as for zeal, persecuting the church; as for legalistic righteousness, faultless.

Philippians 3:4b-6

In my opinion one of the things that made Paul the perfect Apostle to the Gentiles was that he was a devout Jew of all devout Jews. He was a most credible teacher of being under grace and not under the law. And Paul listed in these verses all those "credentials" proving his Jewishness. Ultimately Christ proved and Paul taught for all eternity (through his letters and his teaching) that some things just don't matter.

Credentials are good. Where and how you made your bones is good. Your historical accomplishments are good. But at the end of the day, some things just don't matter. My Lord and Savior was a Jewish carpenter. Paul is wholly responsible for what Christianity is today and he was a Jew. Do you realize the entire New Testament was written by Jewish men except for the Gospel of Luke and Acts?

Some leaders rely too much on their background, too much on their credentials, too much on their resume, and forget what is truly important: helping make their people as successful as they can be.

I didn't say background, credentials, and experiences weren't important. True leaders weigh what really matters in all situations.

CHANGE WHEN YOU KNOW YOU MUST

But whatever was to my profit I now consider loss for the sake of Christ.
Philippians 3:7

This one verse could take you a thousand directions. Paul reiterated the items he listed in verses 4-6 were irrelevant in the big scheme of things. He used to hold all those in the highest regard and now had traded all that for a life of Christ. Some leaders never change for various reasons. I don't believe in changing for change's sake. But when you "know" you must change then you must change.

I know that sounds obvious. But if it's so obvious, why are there endless examples of the opposite? Some leaders are stubborn. Some leaders don't get that they don't get it. Paul was stubborn until the Damascus Road.

The question is: how to know when you "must change?" Pray for wisdom and knowledge. Pray for guidance. Pray for answers. Ask trusted advisors, peers, and friends. Conduct 360 degree assessments on yourself.

True leaders know when change is necessary. True leaders know when the change must happen within.

CORRECTION DOES NOT MEAN CONFLICT

I plead with Euodia and I plead with Syntyche to agree with each other in the Lord.

Philippians 4:2

One of the things about the Bible that is fascinating is how in a Book of 66 Books there are tons of these little gems. Sometimes they are seemingly out of place. Sometimes you wonder if Paul (or the other authors) had a quick tangent thought. You wonder if the scribe put something out of place. As you read a verse, paragraph, or chapter - boom! A verse jumps out at you. I believe every word in the Bible is in the spot it was meant to be.

Here is a verse in which Paul encouraged two folks *to agree with each other in the Lord*. Why would he say this? Who are these two people?

There is a disease in management, and this disease is when supervisors, managers, leaders, etc will not correct behavior. Why do they not correct? I believe one reason of many is that people don't like conflict. I believe another reason is some people just don't care enough. I am not sure what the disagreement was but here is a leader (Paul) encouraging them, pleading with them to agree. Quick, to the point, issue aired, and issue hopefully corrected.

This can only happen when the leader has the courage and confidence to correct, sometimes seemingly inconsequential issues. All correction does not necessarily invoke conflict, in my experience it fixes issues and moves you forward.

PUT WHAT I'VE TAUGHT YOU INTO PRACTICE

Whatever you have learned or received or heard from me, or seen in me—put it into practice. And the God of peace will be with you.

Philippians 4:9

I cannot imagine the amount of money organizations spend annually on training their folks but I'd guess it's in the billions. I'm not a stats guy but I heard (and I'm paraphrasing) that if you attend a class, workshop, seminar, etc. you have about 48 hours to put into practice what you have learned or risk losing 70% of it. I don't know if that stat is accurate but from experience I know that I need to put things I learn into practice or they're gone.

Paul was a consummate trainer, teacher, mentor, professor. His God-inspired words will last an eternity. Mine, not so much. But we can learn a lot from this verse. Read it: *Whatever you have learned or received or heard from me, or seen in me—put it into practice* (emphasis added). Paul knew the senses the human body uses to attain information and knowledge and tried to capitalize on it.

Training dollars are scarce. Training dollars are invaluable if effectively spent. Organizations should maximize every training opportunity and have a deep, broad, and mature follow up process for all their members once returning from training.

If you thought enough to invest the money in a training event, have a process that enables your people to put into practice what they have learned once they've completed it.

SHARING THE GOOD NEWS

All over the world this gospel is bearing fruit and growing, just as it has been doing among you since the day you heard it and understood God's grace in all its truth.

Colossians 1:6b

Paul was the master of articulating big picture facts and how it related to each individual. There is tremendous value in sharing the good news of an organization with the whole organization, as well as, lower level parts and individuals.

From experience people love to hear good news about their company, their teammates, and themselves. It makes you feel special to work in an organization where you are a part of something good or big. Leaders do well when they tout their good news and especially when they tout the good their individuals have done. It's great when you see "testimonies" on a company website naming an individual for a job well done.

There is more buy-in when a leader can articulate what the larger organization is doing and how it relates to each individual. And good leaders show how each individual can impact the overall organization. I know when I work each day, I have an impact on everyone around me, and my impact impacts the organization. I've always felt that way.

True leaders capture that. Christianity has examples of thousands responding to a message (Peter in Acts). It appears more often than not, it is done one believer at a time. Every member in an organization should feel important. True leaders share the good news up and down the chain.

A LEADER'S IMPACT

I want you to know how much I am struggling for you and for those at Laodicea, and for all who have not met me personally.

Colossians 2:1

A leader's impact will be felt by those the leader doesn't even know. That impact can be either positive or negative. Paul's impact has been, is, and will be positively felt by billions of people or more. In some organizations the leader knows everyone and everyone knows him.

In a lot of organizations the inverse is true. That should not matter if the message is true. Paul reminded his readers (even those who had not *personally met* him) that he was *struggling for* them.

Leaders of large companies, nations, or military organizations have a tremendous impact on those under them. In verse 2 Paul talks about his *purpose*. His purpose was ultimately sharing the gospel and he did this as well as anyone in history. Obviously the majority of impact Paul has had and will have is on folks who have never met him.

Leaders don't have to be personally known by their followers to do well and because of that what a phenomenal responsibility and challenge - because a leader's words and deeds are felt by all.

DON'TS

But now you must rid yourselves of all such things as these: anger, rage, malice, slander, and filthy language from your lips.

Colossians 3:8

As I've mentioned, Paul uses "lists" a lot. I'll call this verse "don'ts." There are things I assume at work. I assume my folks will come to work on time. I assume they are competent at the basics of their job. I assume they are loyal to the company. But there are things a leader should not assume and should publicly pronounce.

I'm not a big rules guy. However, I do follow rules. I just don't want a bunch forced on me and I don't force a bunch on my folks. I ascribe to "big boy rules apply." This means be mature and act your age. "Big boy" means I'm not going to worry if you're doing the right thing, I'll know it because you're a "big boy." When you have to articulate expectations, however, there must be no doubt what you want your folks to do or not do.

Christians should not do what Paul says not to do. I have, I do and I will, because I'm human. I'm *under construction* as the t-shirt says. But we should aspire not to do these things.

In a former organization a while back, I actually wrote a policy memo on what my folks were allowed to wear and not allowed to wear while on duty. You may think I am kidding, but I am not. When your folks are doing things they shouldn't, don't assume they know the right thing to do. Tell them what is not acceptable.

Ultimately you want all of your folks to do the right thing when no one is watching. Most people do. Until you get there, there are times when you have to list your don'ts.

ENCOURAGE YOUR CHILDREN

Fathers, do not embitter your children, or they will become discouraged.
Colossians 3:21

Embitter is to make bitter or arouse bitter feelings within someone. I do my best to constantly encourage Meaghan and Sophia. Once you've made someone bitter it's hard and sometimes impossible to get them to respond positively.

We should always encourage our children. Leaders should constantly encourage their folks. We all have tremendous examples of both. When you see folks that have spent a life or a portion of a career in an encouraging environment, that person is probably pretty confident, has high self-esteem, or has a joyous nature. The opposite is true. Folks that have been or are in "bitter" environments mirror what they receive.

Because leaders deal with people and those people have thousands of things on their minds or that they are dealing with over time, leaders are never in perfect environments. However, encouragement is often the best thing we could offer on a consistent basis. This does not mean you don't hold your folks accountable when required, but encouragement is always better than bitterness.

Fathers should encourage their children. True leaders should always choose encouragement over bitterness.

WORKING WITH ALL YOUR HEART

Whatever you do, work at it with all your heart, as working for the Lord, not for men,

Colossians 3:23

We should all be obedient toward God. We should all glorify God in our daily activities. Not everyone is supposed to be a pastor. Not everyone is supposed to be a missionary. More people need to answer their call however. We should all make the most of where we're at in the particular season we are there.

Whether you're a banker, soldier, pastor, athlete, student, *work at it with all your heart*. Even though the majority of us don't make our living in the church we are all witnesses. Paul encouraged his readers and encouraged us to work with all our heart. Because we are not really serving men, we are serving God, and we will be rewarded for it.

I hold in high regard those professionals that work with all their heart toward a common good. I can't stand being around those folks who do whatever just to get by. They are obviously not working for Him.

Most of us have secular bosses that pay us for our labor. Paul taught us to work hard, be honest, and be loyal because those bosses are God-appointed. When we work with all our heart we bring glory to Him.

BRAGGING ABOUT YOUR PEOPLE TO OTHERS

Jesus, who is called Justus, also sends greetings. These are the only Jews among my fellow workers for the kingdom of God, and they have proved a comfort to me.

Colossians 4:11

Along with Justus, Paul credited Aristarchus, Mark and Barnabas as the *only Jews among* his *fellow workers*. Paul had a very challenging mission. Paul dealt with harshness most of us will never experience. Paul was executed for doing his God-given mission. And yet many men distanced themselves because of this harshness. Few stuck by him. Paul bragged about Aristarchus, Mark, and Barnabas to others.

True leaders pass off all credit to their folks. True leaders brag about their people to others. There is tremendous power in complimenting your folks in front of others. A lot of people like getting tangible evidence they are doing well. Examples include plaques, titles, bonuses, accolades.

A lot of people simply want to be acknowledged. They simply want to know what they're doing really matters. When you brag about your folks to others you are giving them in some cases the best compliment you can.

VECTOR CHECK

Tell Archippus: "See to it that you complete the work you have received in the Lord."

Colossians 4:17

A "vector check" is simply confirming you are going in the right direction. You can ask for one, or your boss will give you one without any forewarning. I don't really know what *Archippus' work* was, but obviously it was important because it was *received in the Lord*.

A vector check can simply be an encouraging word or phrase that "you're right on target." Or it can be an acknowledgement of the obvious; *complete the work*. Followers and leaders should want to know if they are on target. Sometimes the only way you know is to ask. Other times your results will prove if you are or not.

Paul was in prison when he wrote this letter. And in the next to last verse of the letter he gave a little shout out to Archippus. Vector checks do not have to be large communiqués. They can simply be a word or short sentence, spoken or written by the leader that acknowledges the follower is on target or gives a course correction.

True leaders do not leave it to chance. They should provide vector checks when necessary.

THANK YOUR PEOPLE

We always thank God for all of you, mentioning you in our prayers.

1 Thessalonians 1:2

Read verse 2 followed by 3. These are a pretty awesome couple of verses. Paul constantly thanked the faithful. "Thank you" are two of the most powerful words you can utter. I think we all could say thank you more.

Thank your people for what they do. I strive to thank my folks early and often for what they do. It can take the form of a private moment, a handwritten note, a public pronouncement, or a literal pat on the back. I know saying thank you is appreciated. I know I appreciate it when someone tells me thank you.

This is one of those little things that mean so much. I don't want to understate what Paul said; he thanked God for the Thessalonians. You don't need to thank God for everything your folks do. True leaders thank their people for all those things they do. Good leaders catch people doing something well and they initiate clear and specific praise. Good leaders also look for ways to publically praise their people.

I knew of a leader who once wanted to give one of his folks an award and, without the individual knowing, informed his family so that the award presentation was witnessed by both coworkers and loved ones. The words and corresponding action acknowledge that their deeds not only are noticed but are appreciated.

BE A MODEL TO EMULATE

You became imitators of us and of the Lord; in spite of severe suffering, you welcomed the message with the joy given by the Holy Spirit. And so you became a model to all the believers in Macedonia and Achaia.

1 Thessalonians 1:6-7

Paul used two great words in these two verses: imitate and *model*. True leaders want and will have others emulate (imitate) them. The responsibility of being a true leader is great. A true leader glorifies God, edifies others, and builds God's Kingdom. This is what we want followers to emulate. Ironically, bad leaders also have followers that emulate them.

You want to be a model that others will emulate. To have this requires first and foremost trust. You also have to have a true message or mission. Also the message or mission has to be for the common good. Your expectations must be clearly articulated. Everything you do must be above reproach.

Remember, you are an example for someone and oftentimes for a lot of people. True leaders know this and embrace the challenge. True leaders are imitated, modeled, and emulated.

CONSTANTLY NURTURE

For you know that we dealt with each of you as a father deals with his own children, encouraging, comforting and urging you to live lives worthy of God, who calls you into his kingdom and glory.

1 Thessalonians 2:11-12

People development is a never-ending process. This process can take many forms, whether you're developing the person's body, mind, or physical competence. People don't magically reach their potential without being nurtured.

Paul described a process like a father dealing with his own children. Leaders who take seriously the nurture and development of their people like that of a parent will be rewarded.

I have found that a person's requirements for nurturing can be wide, varied, and simultaneous. For example a new guy definitely needs job competence nurturing. He may also need some human relationships nurturing. And additionally, he may need some leadership nurturing.

True leaders encourage, comfort, and urge their folks to reach their fullest potential.

SHARED PAIN BRINGS PEOPLE CLOSER TOGETHER

For you, brothers, became imitators of God's churches in Judea, which are in Christ Jesus: You suffered from your own countrymen the same things those churches suffered from the Jews,   1 Thessalonians 2:14

Paul's mission was bringing the gospel to the Gentiles. This letter was to Gentiles. Christianity was born from the Jews. Paul compares the suffering of the Thessalonian *countrymen* and *those churches*. I am convinced that when people go through the same arduous circumstances they grow together.

Through the arduous year and a half of training that it takes to become a Combat Controller, there is a lot of pain and heartache. However, those who share in it are brought closer together. This bond should be maximized. This is one of the reasons sports' teams and the military training at times "breaks them down" only to build them back up. Because once you've built them back up, they are almost unstoppable.

There is also comfort knowing your buddy right next to you is going through the same experiences. Having a buddy to help you through certain sufferings is the only way you can get through. These experiences bring men together.

True leaders capitalize on shared pain. Now remember there may not be any actual physical pain, but if there is a perceived figurative pain or suffering that your followers go through this should be capitalized upon.

BEING AN EXAMPLE

Make it your ambition to lead a quiet life, to mind your own business and to work with your hands, just as we told you, so that your daily life may win the respect of outsiders and so that you will not be dependent on anybody.

1 Thessalonians 4:11-12

Think about all the folks you know that *lead a quiet life, mind* their *own business, work with* their *hands*, and are *not dependent on anybody*. What is one of the first things you would say about them? That they are a good guy? That they are respected? That they are an example to follow?

Paul gave the Thessalonians sound advice. There is a deeper message within these two verses. However, think of these four traits again. These are things I do and aspire to do. And I aspire not to do the opposite. In other words, leaders and followers should not live a "noisy" life. They should not worry about others' issues or be gossips. They should do an honest day's work. And they should be self-sufficient.

I wouldn't feel comfortable following a leader that is the antithesis of any of these four traits. I could argue if you have these four traits you are a good example. True leaders especially follow this advice.

BUILD EACH OTHER UP

Therefore encourage one another and build each other up, just as in fact you are doing.

1 Thessalonians 5:11

This verse follows a great section on the coming of the Lord. Paul encouraged the Thessalonians, who were in the light, that despite the darkness, the sufferings, and anxiety they were experiencing they should continue to build each other up.

The culture of great organizations is full of builders; those that build others up. Simply saying an encouraging word builds each other up. Even strong folks have doubts, anxieties, or are dealing with some form of suffering. Build them up.

Your people will gain trust and feel secure if they are in an environment where they are built up all the time. Eventually, this culture will propel your organization. When someone is convinced of something, it's hard to stop them. If you've done a good job building your folks up, their confidence in themselves and the organization will enable them to deal with life's adversities.

You don't need to tell true leaders to build others up. That is what makes them true leaders.

KNOW YOUR ROLE

Now we ask you, brothers, to respect those who work hard among you, who are over you in the Lord and who admonish you.

1 Thessalonians 5:12

Leaders lead regardless of environment. Leaders have followers. Followers must follow. Not everyone is the commander; there are Airmen and Soldiers who follow their commander. Not everyone in a restaurant is the head chef. You also need waiters, cooks, bus boys, and hostesses. Everyone must know their role.

Leaders lead. Those in an organization must respect those above them who have a job to do. God has no favorites; He loves everyone equally as much. Some positions in some organizations are extremely important. We should all know our role and do our role for the common good.

True leaders know they need people to accomplish their organization's mission. True leaders also know how to motivate the head chef as well as the bus boy. True leaders get their folks to understand and buy in to their role.

When Michael Jordan played for the Chicago Bulls there was no doubt that he was the leader of the team. But when Steve Kerr or John Paxson came off the bench they knew they needed to bang down a three when the circumstances presented themselves. Know your role.

ACKNOWLEDGE PERSEVERANCE

Therefore, among God's churches we boast about your perseverance and faith in all the persecutions and trials you are enduring.

2 Thessalonians 1:4

Nothing significant would have gotten done in history without perseverance. Men and women who persevere are special. Those who persevere are rare. Leaders need to acknowledge their folks that persevere. Leaders need to encourage their folks to persevere despite obstacles.

When I look at the traits I want in my people; character, initiative, resourcefulness, reliability and perseverance top the list. Leaders can only do so much toward mission accomplishment. Their folks must have a certain amount of personal perseverance.

If things were always easy we probably would not have such a strong need for leaders. If things were always easy, perseverance would probably not be required. That is what makes it so special: it's a rarity.

True leaders acknowledge perseverance. And true leaders develop a hiring process to find those with it or develop a system to nurture it once you've hired your folks.

REITERATE SOUND DOCTRINE

We have confidence in the Lord that you are doing and will continue to do the things we command.

2 Thessalonians 3:4

Without Paul a lot of people would not have received the gospel. A lot of people first heard the gospel from Paul. Paul knew "the" gospel was "the" gospel not "a" gospel. He knew he had delivered sound doctrine to the Thessalonians. And he reminded them to stick to it (verses 1-3).

In verse 4 he reiterated his *confidence* they were *doing and* would *continue to do the things* he *commanded*. Paul constantly reminded young converts to focus on the gospel. He reminded his young converts to stick with sound doctrine; what he had taught.

I'm a huge believer in the basics. The gospel is one of the basics of Christianity. If you chose to reiterate things, lean toward the basics. The basics in everything form the foundation. If you have a strong foundation, a lot of things can be built upon that.

True leaders reiterate sound doctrine. I've taught in countless seminars that once you've developed your one, two, few or whatever "core" beliefs, keep hammering them home. Then remind your folks of your confidence in sticking to them.

EXCEEDING THE STANDARD

nor did we eat anyone's food without paying for it. On the contrary, we worked night and day, laboring and toiling so that we would not be a burden to any of you.

2 Thessalonians 3:8

As an Apostle, Paul was authorized to be financially and logistically taken care of by believers. It appeared he always paid his own way and worked for what he needed. Paul knew his message would be the most credible if while he delivered it, he exceeded all standards. He never asked what he didn't expect of himself.

Leaders are more credible when they practice "do what I do" versus "do what I say." Paul was also teaching not to be idle. Christians should be about our Lord's business. Paul literally trekked thousands of miles, made a living by making tents, probably didn't take hand outs, probably slept little, and otherwise made the most of every minute of every day fulfilling his mission.

It's amazing how easy it is to follow someone who does all those little things. It's easy to follow someone who exceeds every standard. It's easy to follow someone who can be counted on no matter what.

You all have heard the axiom "work smarter not harder." I believe it myself. However, there is a lot to be said about those that *work night and day, laboring and toiling so that* you are *not a burden* on anyone. There is a lot to be said about hard work. True leaders lead from the front and exceed the standard.

PEER PRESSURE WORKS

If anyone does not obey our instruction in this letter, take special note of him. Do not associate with him, in order that he may feel ashamed. Yet do not regard him as an enemy, but warn him as a brother.

2 Thessalonians 3:14-15

This is sound teaching. We're to love everyone but we're not to enable willful sinners or those that do not believe. A way to get some teammates that aren't on the same page is through peer pressure. Peer pressure works. This assumes the person/people in question has/have potential.

I spent 21+ years in a highly selective, extremely unique, elite environment. There were times when the boss couldn't or shouldn't get involved in certain issues. In most of those cases he either expected or implied the team would take care of those who didn't obey (so to speak). When you have a bunch of men all on the same page and one or a very few not getting it, the peer pressure exerted by the bunch was invaluable.

Remember this assumes the person had potential. If they didn't get that they didn't get it and never would, you have to cut them away. If they had potential, then more often than not peer pressure would work.

I know this might sound unbiblical, but think about it. You are still *warning him as a brother*. So he has to be a brother. If he's not, you shouldn't consort with him or enable him. In real good organizations you'll have very few of these issues. If you are a great organization, you'll have a very tiny fraction of these.

True leaders ensure their highly mature teams use peer pressure when needed.

NEVER TIRE OF DOING WHAT IS RIGHT

And as for you, brothers, never tire of doing what is right.

2 Thessalonians 3:13

This is near the end of a section warning against idleness. It appeared some Thessalonians thought the second coming was very near and were just chilling out waiting. Paul warned against this.

As far as "the right thing to do" for Christians, it appears easier now that we have the whole Bible to know what He expects of us. Think about it, so much back then was word of mouth. And in certain environments, things we would view as totally reprehensible were viewed as okay back then. So Paul and others would preach and teach the gospel. And the New Testament didn't even exist back then. So the "right thing" was what they were told it was. And there were lots of false teachers and others trying to corrupt Paul's message.

Here he urged them to *never tire of doing what* was *right*. However you received *what is right*: a checklist, a book, a memorandum, or words from someone; never tire of doing what is right. How do you get people to do this? First you have to inform them of what is right. Provide examples of what right has done for someone else. Capitalize on a group doing what is right and encourage others to follow. Constantly reiterate what is right. Encourage your people to do what is right. Correct when you have to.

True leaders never tire of doing what is right. And true leaders get groups of people to do the same.

A PURE HEART

The goal of this command is love, which comes from a pure heart and a good conscience and a sincere faith.

1 Timothy 1:5

Timothy was Paul's protégé. Paul constantly taught Timothy. In verses 3 and 4 he warned Timothy against false teachers. Paul said *the goal of this command is love*. A lot of times it's not what is said but how it is said. What comes out of your mouth is normally what is in your heart. You can only love or have language that builds up if you have *a pure heart*.

I am a big failure in this area. Please do not think that I am perfect, I know most of you don't.

A pure heart can only come if the Spirit is in you. Language that edifies can only come from a pure heart. Good leaders can correct without unwholesome talk (Eph 4:29). They can disagree without being disagreeable. As much as you might want to return garbage with the same, respond out of love.

How do you respond with a pure heart? Like I said, you have to have the Spirit within you; you must be a believer. Pray for wisdom and knowledge. Know your subject or the issue well enough to articulate without emotion. Take a second to respond.

True leaders have a pure heart. They don't respond out of anger but try to respond out of love.

HE IS IN CHARGE

I thank Christ Jesus our Lord, who has given me strength, that he considered me faithful, appointing me to his service.

1 Timothy 1:12

Paul knew he was one of the greatest of sinners. He and Luke articulate this in various places. As I've mentioned, Paul was perhaps the perfect person to undertake this mission. He was a horrible persecutor of the church and became the greatest promoter of the gospel.

Paul was thankful for being *appointed to His service*. Once Paul saw the truth I believe he tried harder than most would have ever tried, knowing where he had came from. I don't believe God measures the size of the sin like humans do, but Paul did. He was humble that God *considered* him *faithful*.

I believe most of my mature adult life I was where God wanted me to be. I take seriously where I'm at now. I will always take serious where God puts me. I am in His service and He is in charge. I still have problems with the flesh and my own personal desires but I know He is in charge.

True leaders know He's in charge. Once you realize that, your service to Him and to your organization will be pure.

WHERE HAVE YOU BEEN

But for that very reason I was shown mercy so that in me, the worst of sinners, Christ Jesus might display his unlimited patience as an example for those who would believe on him and receive eternal life.

1 Timothy 1:16

There are about 52 messages in this verse. A huge one is no one can fathom the patience of God. Again, one of the things that made Paul so great was where he had been. Jesus didn't come to save the righteous; He came to save the sinners. Paul described himself as *the worst of sinners* (Verses 15 and 16). Then he described Jesus' *mercy* and *unlimited patience* and how He used himself *as an example.*

I think there is a certain amount of validation or credibility in where someone has been. In some cases a leader is more respected when he's worked his way up the chain. I do not say you must work your way up to become a great leader. Bill Parcells, although drafted, never played in the NFL, yet was a great coach and General Manager. When the leader has been through the trenches he has earned a certain amount of credibility.

Where you have been means you've been there, done that. We're all sinners. I don't celebrate where I am compared to where I was on the sin spectrum. I celebrate that I am saved and try to be obedient. Where have you been means that you cannot only talk the talk, but also walk the walk. Followers want to know where you've been.

If you have great leadership qualities AND you've worked your way up the chain, your followers will respect you just a bit more.

QUALITIES OF LEADERS

Here is a trustworthy saying: If anyone sets his heart on being an overseer, he desires a noble task. Now the overseer must be above reproach, the husband of but one wife, temperate, self-controlled, respectable, hospitable, able to teach, not given to drunkenness, not violent but gentle, not quarrelsome, not a lover of money. He must manage his own family well and see that his children obey him with proper respect. (If anyone does not know how to manage his own family, how can he take care of God's church?) He must not be a recent convert, or he may become conceited and fall under the same judgment as the devil. He must also have a good reputation with outsiders, so that he will not fall into disgrace and into the devil's trap.

1 Timothy 3:1-7

The reason I left you in Crete was that you might straighten out what was left unfinished and appoint elders in every town, as I directed you. An elder must be blameless, the husband of but one wife, a man whose children believe and are not open to the charge of being wild and disobedient. Since an overseer is entrusted with God's work, he must be blameless—not overbearing, not quick-tempered, not given to drunkenness, not violent, not pursuing dishonest gain. Rather he must be hospitable, one who loves what is good, who is self-controlled, upright, holy and disciplined. He must hold firmly to the trustworthy message as it has been taught, so that he can encourage others by sound doctrine and refute those who oppose it.

Titus 1:5-9

In my introduction I commented that there are thousands of books on leadership. Paul, inspired by God, wrote some of the best. Every book on leadership has lists of qualities and traits. And 1Timothy and Titus are no exception. Even my first book had them. During a seminar that I present a lot, I have a full page of qualities and traits of a leader I hand out and discuss.

Read and reflect on these two passages. Sounds like a person I would like to hang out with. The people Paul describes are leaders at home, at church, and in public. He describes a person that Jesus instructed us to be like. These qualities include a focus on discipline, professionalism, humility, maturity, and being a good example.

Anyone can easily write a list of perceived qualities of a leader. True leaders live by these qualities and more.

LEADERS MUST BE ABOVE REPROACH

Now the overseer must be above reproach, the husband of but one wife, temperate, self-controlled, respectable, hospitable, able to teach,

1 Timothy 3:2

I was in a "Coaching" class while in my current job and when we were asked to introduce ourselves one of the requirements was to describe our leadership philosophy. Most people answered appropriately. The first thing I said was that I seek to live in such a way as to be above reproach in everything. I went on to describe "everything." It included my character, competence, commitment, daily activities, my appearance, demeanor, etc; everything must be and is above reproach.

This is before you can describe any sort of philosophy. If you can't be a follower, you can't be a leader. If you don't exude self-discipline, you can't be a leader. If you are to lead you must first start with yourself.

Now realize we are humans and as such imperfect. That's not an excuse, and I am not naïve; I know I have lots of room for improvement. Your daily activities are a function of what you made them out to be and in essence what your environment expects. Aristotle said, "We are what we repeatedly do. Excellence then, is not an act, but a habit." Being above criticism is a habit.

I've said repeatedly that a leader must have integrity and his trustworthiness equals his credibility. It does not matter how much he is liked or how competent he is or how charismatic he is; if he can't be trusted he can't lead.

I practice what I preach. I live my values. I expect a lot out of my people and expect more out of myself. True leaders are above reproach.

LEADERSHIP IS A NOBLE TASK

Here is a trustworthy saying: If anyone sets his heart on being an overseer, he desires a noble task.

1 Timothy 3:1

Leadership is a noble task. Remember in *Armageddon*, Harry, Bruce Willis' character, asked (and I'm paraphrasing), "The United States government just asked us to help save the planet. Who is going to turn them down?" When leaders are asked to lead, they lead. I don't think Harry wanted to be asked, but he was, and he answered the call.

When you know you're a leader, you don't necessarily advertise that you want a certain job or position. However, you know you're a leader, and when asked, you'll do the noble thing, if of course taking the position is the right thing to do. I've set my heart on being a leader. I try to reach my potential everyday and work at it every day.

The reason leadership is such a noble task is because it involves people. Regardless of where the leader actually is, he is leading people to accomplish some task or ongoing mission. The reason leadership is so critical, is because, relatively speaking, leaders are in short supply and leading people is so important.

Leadership is a noble task. You should take the responsibility seriously. True leaders are humble and ready when they see a need to influence or answer the call to lead.

REPUTATION IS WHAT OTHERS SAY ABOUT YOU

He must also have a good reputation with outsiders, so that he will not fall into disgrace and into the devil's trap.

1 Timothy 3:7

Have you ever wondered what others say about you? That is what reputation is. It's how you are known, it's how you are viewed, and it's a barometer of your character. How do you build *a good reputation?* It takes time and involves doing *good* things in public as well as private. Ironically, reputation, like character, can be viewed positively and negatively. You are known as a certain type of person, which is your reputation…good or bad.

Paul instructed Timothy to have *a good reputation with outsiders.* There appears to be some people that spend their time looking for your warts or chinks in your armor so they can validate their hypocrisy. Let's say you're a leader and some folks are not on board. If they find they can show you have a bad reputation, this may be a way they can start chipping away at your credibility.

Reputation takes years to build and validate, and can be lost quite easily. True leaders have a good reputation and are constantly proving it.

LEADERS MUST BE TESTED

They must first be tested; and then if there is nothing against them, let them serve as deacons.

1 Timothy 3:10

I was asked in one of my seminars if anyone is allowed to think they are a leader. I answered it this way: Yes. Then I qualified my response: if an environment involves people, and leadership is needed, then a leader must step up. This is regardless of anyone's formal position. In concert with my born/made comments in the introduction, leaders must be able and willing.

Ability includes: knowledge (do they know how); experience (have they done it); and skill (are they doing it now). Willingness includes: confidence (can they do it); commitment (will they do it); and motivation (do they want to do it). Don't confuse motivation with ability. Don't confuse enthusiasm with motivation or ability.

As leaders grow, hopefully they are in an environment that allows them to grow. Some environments can allow their growing leaders to make mistakes. You will grow with nurturing and by learning from your mistakes. For certain positions a leader must have been tested before he can be considered the leader.

To put it bluntly, you don't want a rookie leading your entire organization. A leader must have ability and willingness which includes six sub-characteristics. To get to that level a leader must be tested and proven worthy. True leaders have a proven process to test their lower level leaders along the maturation process.

OVERCOME YOUTH WITH EXAMPLE

Don't let anyone look down on you because you are young, but set an example for the believers in speech, in life, in love, in faith and in purity.

1 Timothy 4:12

I've been in a leadership environment since 1985 (not counting high school). I've been a leader in certain circumstances and was considered young. A lot of my leadership experiences were apropos based on my age and environment. However, when you're young for the position you are in, you have to overcome a perception with some people. A way to do this is by setting the example or being the example.

Paul reminded Timothy to *set an example* in all that he did. Being the example includes being above reproach in all things. There cannot be any doubt in your commitment. There cannot be any doubt in your motives. There cannot be any doubt in your integrity. In essence, when you're young and a leader you have to make up for your lack of experience. You do this by ensuring all the other areas are good to go.

Remember what Aristotle said…excellence in your daily activities will become a habit. Eventually you will do those things long and consistently enough and they become what you do. When you are young you should maximize every opportunity to learn as much as you can not only about the issue but about the leadership necessary to lead in it.

People follow leaders regardless of age for a lot of reasons, including but not limited to, trust, respect, inspiration, charisma, and example. The example you set will become a part of your daily activities and will aid your growth as you mature. Be the example, especially if you're a young leader.

FAITH, FAMILY AND EVERYTHING ELSE

If anyone does not provide for his relatives, and especially for his immediate family, he has denied the faith and is worse than an unbeliever.

1 Timothy 5:8

Your priorities should be God, your family, and then everything else. I've put work above my family and above my faith more than I care to acknowledge. I guess everyone has at times. It does not matter how awesome you are at work if you suck as a Dad. I heard Max Lucado say, "In parenting, there are no mulligans." All of your accolades from work pale when compared to when your wife knows you don't measure up as a husband. You are not faithful if you do not care for your family.

No one ever says on their death bed, "I wish I spent more time at work." It appears when we truly have time to reflect we all realize the importance of our faith and our family. There is obviously a balance between all that we do. When you're in the military for example you can't say "no" to the boss when he needs you to deploy, when you know it will cut into your family time. But when your family is always last, always second to everything else you are *denying the faith*.

The only way to make your family a priority is to have Christ in your heart. When you truly live as He wants you to, being a good Husband or good Dad is never a question. Every once in a while you need to assess your priorities: Faith, Family and everything else. I would say your ministry and your career are priorities three and four, respectively. Interestingly, when your priorities are in order your family life is probably as good as it can be.

Leaders have a huge responsibility. True leaders put their faith first, then their family, and then everything else. It's only because they keep their priorities in order that they can be considered true leaders.

GUARD WHAT HAS BEEN ENTRUSTED

Timothy, guard what has been entrusted to your care. Turn away from godless chatter and the opposing ideas of what is falsely called knowledge,
1 Timothy 6:20

I love that Paul used Timothy's name in this verse; it makes it more personal. Timothy was *entrusted* with leading the church at Ephesus (in this letter). The "*what*" Timothy was entrusted with was the truth of the gospel. Leaders are entrusted with the care of their mission and their people. We must guard that against all things.

Paul cautioned against *godless chatter* and false teachers. In a lot of environments leaders don't have to worry about those set against him. They just don't exist. They normally just have to worry about normal environmental factors. There are times when men of ill repute and demonic forces are against you. You must guard against this.

An unrivaled commitment to mission completion is important. Prayer to do His will and prayer for strength and courage is more important. Following His example will help you through your tough times.

True leaders guard their mission and their people against as much as possible. Focus on your mission and take care of your people and don't let obstacles and naysayers stand in your way. What you do is important… guard it.

A GOOD SOLDIER

Endure hardship with us like a good soldier of Christ Jesus.
                                                          2 Timothy 2:3

The word "soldier" has certain connotations. I was privileged to be an Airman in the United States Air Force for 21+ years and I can identify with "soldier." The old commercial said, "A soldier never takes the easy way out." Or these: "A soldier does more before 9 AM than most people do all day," "An Army of One," and most recently, "Army strong."

A soldier (every service member) endures many things: deployments, no-notice changes in work hours, the elements, missing lots of family time, physical danger, competing priorities, etc. A soldier must be strong: physically, mentally, spiritually, and psychologically. If we have Christ within, we have all we need if we know how to lean on Him.

I've felt some hardships. I've endured some hardships. I, however, am the least of the men I served with. I am thoroughly amazed what we ask our Airmen, Soldiers, Marines, Sailors, and Coastguardsmen to do, and more amazed at what they actually do. They never fail to impress.

I use the word soldier as a synonym for all those in the military. When Americans look at a Soldier they may think they know what he does and has gone through. Some know, others assume, few have lived it. A miniscule population truly understands the hardship a Soldier endures. That's not right or wrong, that's just the way it is. A grateful and free nation thanks you.

LEADERS MUST DEVELOP OTHERS LEADERS

And the things you have heard me say in the presence of many witnesses entrust to reliable men who will also be qualified to teach others.

2 Timothy 2:2

Leaders must develop other leaders. When you develop followers, you build your organization one person at a time; when you develop leaders you force multiply your organization. True leaders develop those around them.

To be successful on a consistent, persistent, long-term basis, organizations must develop their talent. They must develop from within and have a process to attract external talent. True leaders are secure enough with themselves, that they ultimately should be grooming folks to replace themselves. Paul described *reliable men* who should *be qualified*. The leaders in an organization determine the process for their own leader development. They should determine when someone is reliable enough and qualified enough to be considered the leader.

There are many reasons the culture in Special Tactics is that of excellence. One of the main reasons is there is an objective, logical, identifiable process to develop leaders within. Mark Scholl told me once that the hole your foot leaves when you take it out of a bucket of water is how much you'll be missed when you're gone. Meaning, everyone is expendable. Don't take this out of context. If you're not secure enough to know your organization will keep on trucking when you're gone, you probably aren't a true leader.

All organizations, especially those in the military, have turnover. To ensure the organization stays successful mandates a full and trained cadre of leaders. True leaders develop the leaders around them. It's the only way to keep an organization on a positive path over time.

PLEASING THE LEADER

No one serving as a soldier gets involved in civilian affairs—he wants to please his commanding officer.

2 Timothy 2:4

Paul used a great metaphor: the soldier. Remember, when he was in prison or held captive (on more than a few occasions) he was with and around Roman soldiers. Please read Ephesians 6 again. I want to focus on the phrase, *"to please his commanding officer."* If you're in an organization that "gets it," you are around a lot of people that want to be there. And if you want to be in an organization, you want to please the leader.

In the American military there is an adage: "We don't practice democracy, we defend it." And most of us bought into that. It doesn't mean there aren't extremely bright, intellectual, and articulate military citizens that vote and speak their mind. But a soldier knows to stay out of politics.

To get your folks to please you, it helps to start with a motivated, disciplined, and professional group that has bought into your program, but more importantly, bought into you. I wanted to please most leaders that were over me. I know now that authorities are destined by God. The leaders that I truly trusted and respected got my 100% commitment. I tried to go out of my way to please them.

I was always motivated by what was the right thing to do, what was good for the team, and I did what I was supposed to do. Because of all that, I was personally rewarded. I hope you've experienced it or can imagine what it's like when you're in an organization where everyone is on the same page and do their jobs because they want to.

STEER CLEAR OF FOOLS AND STUPIDITY

Don't have anything to do with foolish and stupid arguments, because you know they produce quarrels.

2 Timothy 2:23

Remember this is Paul's advice to Timothy. I wish more leaders would not entertain *foolish and stupid arguments*. I categorize these as those you know are not right, not true, or are negatively motivated. I didn't and don't have anything to do with fools or stupidity. If I know I'm right and know my motives are for the good of the cause, it's irrelevant what a fool has to say. I steer clear of such.

As I've matured as a leader I've become more empathetic. Not as much as some people wish, but I have become more tolerant of things. Allowing foolish and stupid arguments wastes time, could misuse resources, is bad for morale, and could create dissension. Leaders nip it in the bud right away.

Some immature leaders may not clearly see a well thought out, or articulated argument or issue, by a seemingly squared away guy, as what it is: foolishness or stupidity. This could happen especially if the leader is new. Think about it, if you're new and you ask questions from your "experienced" guys you may not know they're a fool or stupid.

I am speaking plainly and don't want to sound unbiblical or unchristian. True leaders know their environment. True leaders have the filter to see through foolishness or stupid arguments and lead the organization the right way.

LEADERS ARE ALWAYS PREPARED

Preach the Word; be prepared in season and out of season; correct, rebuke and encourage—with great patience and careful instruction.

2 Timothy 4:2

This is some of the soundest advice in the Bible in my opinion. Paul instructed Timothy to be ready at all times to preach the Word. He also reminded Timothy that the Word (the Old Testament in this case) was good to correct, rebuke and encourage.

Paul didn't tell Timothy to only be ready on Sundays or Bible Studies or Sunday school. He told him to be prepared in and out of season (at all times). True leaders are prepared at all times. And they have their core values and core mission always ready.

I've heard a man say that if you make all decisions based on your values then no decision is hard. This assumes your values are good and of a high standard. If you can always be counted on to do the right thing and always be counted on to maintain the standard, you'll never have any issues beyond your control.

Regardless of environment, situation, or who is around, leaders are always prepared to lead the right way.

GOING ALL THE WAY

For I am already being poured out like a drink offering, and the time has come for my departure. I have fought the good fight, I have finished the race, I have kept the faith.

2 Timothy 4:6-7

I can't imagine what it's like to know you're about to be executed. But Paul knew to die was to gain (in Christ). Paul kept his composure all the way to the end. God told him he would go to Rome (Acts 23:11) and he did. God told Paul he would suffer for Him (Acts 9:16) and he did.

A true leader has what it takes to go all the way. Not all environments call for a man to go to his death for his ideals - but some do. A true leader will inspire followers when they see that he is willing to go all the way.

STAND STRONG EVEN IF BY YOURSELF

At my first defense, no one came to my support, but everyone deserted me. May it not be held against them.

2 Timothy 4:16

It appears this was written in Paul's so called second Roman imprisonment. And it appears he knew he was about to be executed. In this second letter to Timothy, Paul informed Timothy that it appeared no one supported him in his defense. At this time, people had, and were continuing to desert Paul, due to the apparent pain experienced by being seen as his supporter.

During this period when you were an enemy of the state (so to speak) those that followed you or appeared to support you would also come under the scrutiny or punishment of the state, possibly including death. It appears Paul's followers quit, or ran away, kept their distance, or attempted to protect their own skin. They left Paul fending for himself.

A man's character is sometimes built during adversity, but it is always revealed. Want to know the true character of a man, watch him when everything around him is in a state of chaos. Paul stood strong despite being alone (or with seemingly few friends by his side).

True leaders stand strong even when they are by themselves.

ENCOURAGE AND REBUKE WITH AUTHORITY

These, then, are the things you should teach. Encourage and rebuke with all authority. Do not let anyone despise you.

Titus 2:15

I try my best to build others up through encouragement. I also know when correction is required. At times my assessment and actions have been wrong; I did not encourage when I should have, or I corrected when I did not have to. The authority I have, had either been earned or sometimes was a work in progress. A true leader's encouragement and rebuke have a lot more impact based on the amount of authority he possesses.

Authority is built over time. It's built from doing what is right no matter what. It's built by focusing on truth. And it's built by having character above reproach. Followers don't expect their leaders to know everything in the world. But they do expect to be inspired. They expect to be led. And they expect to be encouraged often and corrected when appropriate.

True leaders have authority. They act and speak with authority. Use your authority to add value to your organization.

LEADERS DELEGATE

The reason I left you in Crete was that you might straighten out what was left unfinished and appoint elders in every town, as I directed you.

Titus 1:5

A friend of mine, Andy Cobb, used to say "a good leader is a good delegator." I used to think I could do it all. As I got more mature I realized I can do a lot, but I can't do everything. Good leaders train their replacements, develop other leaders, nurture growth on their teams or in their organizations so when the need for other leaders is required, they're ready.

To delegate requires the person to be able and willing. It doesn't do any good to delegate a job to an unqualified person or someone lacking in the confidence and/or motivation to get the job done. To be as effective as you can be requires you to delegate. Leaders are paid to do the heavy lifting, to make the big decisions, to be out front; these require you to be able to delegate a lot of things.

To delegate does not mean fire and forget. Situational leadership mandates that you lead folks based on their readiness. To delegate does not mean you give someone a task then micromanage them. To delegate means you have turned over the responsibility and accountability of a task, issue, or mission to someone. It also means you've provided appropriate guidance, as well as milestone, communication, and end state requirements.

If you can't delegate, it's either because you are a micromanager and do not want to relinquish control, which means you are an ineffective leader and need to change. Or, you have not properly developed your people, and that means you are an ineffective leader and need to change. Both of these are fixable. Leaders force multiply.

Develop leaders around you so delegation becomes natural and allows you to make the most impact in your critical areas of influence.

DO THE BASICS EXTRAORDINARILY WELL

He must hold firmly to the trustworthy message as it has been taught, so that he can encourage others by sound doctrine and refute those who oppose it.

Titus 1:9

He refers back to the *overseer* (depending on your Bible version); and Paul instructed Titus what to do on Crete. The *trustworthy message* is the gospel and was *taught* by Paul and others. *Doctrine* is a codification of beliefs, a body of teachings, a particular group of philosophies, principles, or procedures, and as such is the basics of any field. This was one of Paul's often-used instructions. There is only one gospel. And according to Paul we must *hold firmly* to it.

There are plenty of environments that are extremely complex and detailed. However, the majority of environments are made up of people doing the basics. What separates the superstars? The superstars know and do the basics extraordinarily well. This includes when your folks not only know but live the vision, mission, and values of your organization. When you see an "expert" in his field and if you truly watch what he does and believes in, it's nothing more than the basics done extraordinarily well.

I don't mean to oversimplify by stating doctrine is the basics, but it is. You have got to know what the foundational things are for your organization, your work center, and your job. When you truly analyze them, they will include a ton of doctrinal or basic things.

True leaders make sure their folks know the organization's doctrine. They make sure they teach it early and often. They ensure it is followed. Successful people and organizations do the basics extraordinarily well.

BE AN EXAMPLE FOR YOUNG PEOPLE

In everything set them an example by doing what is good. In your teaching show integrity, seriousness and soundness of speech that cannot be condemned, so that those who oppose you may be ashamed because they have nothing bad to say about us.

Titus 2:7-8

Verses 7 and 8 refer back to verse 6 with respect to *young men*. Remember, a ton is taught to young people (especially our kids) through examples set by older more mature folks. You want to make sure the example you set is good and not the bad example a lot of us set. Good fruit comes from good trees. Leading and training young people are phenomenal responsibilities. I take them extremely seriously.

Paul instructed, "*In your teaching show integrity, seriousness and soundness of speech.*" I cannot overemphasize the importance of integrity in everything you do. I've experienced it first-hand and have reiterated it throughout this book, if you do not have integrity you will not be a credible leader regardless of anything else you possess. Take what you do seriously, but do not take yourself too seriously. I take what I do seriously. You can't be a true leader by treating your responsibility like a hobby. And what comes out of your mouth should be sound, should be true, and should be edifying.

Young people will look to leaders for the right thing to do. And depending on the environment, they also look to leaders for what they can get away with. You'll get what you expect. Expect high standards. Expect excellence. Be the example, especially to young people.

I have mentors that I've relied on throughout my life. I still call some of them for advice and counsel that I've known for over 20 years. I am still called for advice and counsel by those who've known me for over 20 years. These relationships have been built amongst other things on the examples set by the older leader.

INSTRUCTIONS WITH DIVISIVE PEOPLE

Warn a divisive person once, and then warn him a second time. After that, have nothing to do with him.

Titus 3:10

This verse is talking about believers and unbelievers. But there is a powerful lesson. I can't count how many times a leader would spend valuable, irreplaceable time trying to get a guy on board. Sometimes you just need to cut your losses. An empathetic, positive or compassionate leader will do everything in his power to get someone on his page: compromise, build consensus, nurture, etc.

However, there are times when doing all that is not worth it. If you know your objective is clear and you've got your team on board and you have someone not getting on board, drop him, fire him, cut him, or whatever is the term in your world. Don't sacrifice the bigger picture for a divisive person.

APPEAL IN A WAY ASIDE FROM RANK

Therefore, although in Christ I could be bold and order you to do what you ought to do,

Philemon 8

Paul had Apostolic authority. As such he could have "ordered" Philemon to take Onesimus back without debate. Using rank almost never results in a positive outcome. Overuse, just like overusing any tool in your toolbox, will dilute its effectiveness. True leaders never focus on position power. True leaders focus on personal power. Paul had personal power.

A question should be: "Can I accomplish what I need to, positively?" If the answer is "Yes," then attempt it. In my experience, when I've actually thought about this, the outcome was way better than "Because I said so!"

I feel some leaders and leadership schools of thought expect you to never use the negative or less than positive methods. The military, sports teams, intense environments all have proven that at times strong-willed, "my way or the highway," works.

It's not the best method in all situations but it is a method. Strive to not lean on your rank or authority. Remember, in a lot of situations (some may say all) it's not what you say, it's how you say it.

WE'RE ALL USEFUL FOR SOMEONE

Formerly he was useless to you, but now he has become useful both to you and to me.

Philemon 11

Onesimus means *useful*. Paul had an excellent play on words in his letter to Philemon. Remember in the first century AD, slavery was a part of the culture. At this point in time (rule of the entire Mediterranean basin by Rome) slaves were a hugely important and accepted aspect of life. Also, Paul and other spreaders of the gospel did not want to embitter Roman sensibilities by denouncing slavery: not yet anyway.

Slaves that did something wrong against their owner knew they would be punished or killed, depending on the severity. Apparently Onesimus did something wrong with his owner Philemon. He may have perhaps stolen something. And it appeared he ran away, possibly to Rome, and while there encountered Paul and was probably saved and became a great help to Paul; in essence, Onesimus became his Christian brother.

Now Paul was nothing if not practical. He knew that just because Onesimus was saved did not negate his crime. Christians are supposed to love their neighbor. Paul tried to appeal to Philemon by reminding him that Onesimus had become useful in his (Paul's) ministry. This would also remind Philemon that Paul was present when Philemon accepted Jesus as his personal Lord and savior.

When a true leader vouches for someone else, even if that other person has done something unpopular, wrong, etc, it enables the person to be received by others more positively. However, that person needs to prove or re-prove himself worthy. But the leader's vouching opens the door.

THE SILVER LINING

Perhaps the reason he was separated from you for a little while was that you might have him back for good—

Philemon 15

It's implied that Onesimus had done something bad toward Philemon. Somehow he found Paul and became saved. And as a servant of Paul's, Onesimus was now doing well for him. Paul's point is out of the bad action, *good* amounted. Onesimus was separated from Philemon but was returning better and for *good*.

Some times there is a silver lining. Things happen for a reason. True leaders can salvage a lot out of seemingly bad situations. Paul did this with Onesimus.

APPEALING TO A MAN'S HEART AND CHARACTER

Confident of your obedience, I write to you, knowing that you will do even more than I ask.

Philemon 21

I believe Paul was the master of saying the right words in the right manner to get his desired effect. Some might want to argue that Paul used reverse psychology in verse 21. I don't. I believe Paul truly appealed to Philemon's heart and to his character.

If you know your people truly know the right thing to do and the big picture, you know given the right encouragement, they will always do the right thing. Most people want to do good. Most people want to do what is right. Most people want to know they matter.

Read the verse again: *"Confident of your obedience…knowing that you will do even more than I ask."* If you have truly built others up and edified them, they will want to do things for you. Paul showed his confidence in Philemon. He knew Philemon would do even more than he asked. Paul knew because of Philemon's heart and this perfectly articulated letter, love would reign. Is that awesome or what?

Without playing games, true leaders should appeal to a man's heart when appropriate. Crafted in the right manner the potential of your people and organization is nearly limitless.

PART 3

CONCLUSION

Paul was a true leader. During his ministry he glorified God, he edified others, and he built God's Kingdom. He had a very challenging mission, yet did as well as anyone could have. He suffered to serve God. He brought Christianity further than anyone.

When you read through Acts and Paul's thirteen letters you'll see leadership nuggets throughout. Leaders lead regardless of environment. Leaders focus on their mission and take care of their people. True leaders love people and know that through people, objectives are accomplished.

I don't know if Paul got down or got frustrated during his ministry. I can only assume he did. There have been times when I have gotten down or gotten frustrated, but like Paul I never quit and I will never quit leading to the best of my ability. Leadership is a phenomenal responsibility that I take extremely seriously. After all, I believe I am in the position of leadership God wants me to be at this particular time.

SELECTED SCRIPTURE

INTRODUCTION:

Jer 1:4-5   Gal 1:15   Psa 139:13

MISSION:

Acts 9:15-16   Rom 11:13-14   Eph 1:1
Acts 13:2   Rom 15:15-16   Eph 3:1-3
Acts 14:26   1 Cor 1:1   Eph 3:7-8
Acts 18:9-10   1 Cor 9:1-2   Col 1:25
Acts 20:24   2 Cor 1:1   1 Thes 2:4
Acts 22:14-15   2 Cor 13:10   1 Tim 1:1
Acts 22:21   Gal 1:1   1 Tim 2:7
Acts 23:11   Gal 1:11-12   2 Tim 1:11
Acts 26:15-18   Gal 1:15-16   Titus 1:3
Rom 1:1   Gal 2:7-8

LESSONS:

Acts	21:13	4:9
9:23-25	23:11	4:16
9:27	24:2-3	4:17
13:11-12	24:24-26	5:6-7
13:16	25:11	6:6
13:46-47	26:1-3	9:21
13:51	28:31	9:27
14:15	**Romans**	10:17
14:19b	1:9	12:7
14:22	2:6	12:12
14:23	2:7	12:18
14:27-28	2:8	12:22
15:2	5:3-4	12:26
15:32	8:29-30	14:40
15:36	12:2	15:9
15:38	12:6	15:33
16:25	12:10	15:58
17:2-4	12:17	16:13
17:22-23	12:18	**2 Corinthians**
18:5-6	13:10	1:3-4
18:9-10	15:15	1:17
19:9-10	16:17	4:16
19:26	**1 Corinthians**	6:9
20:7	1:1	6:14
20:23-24	1:10	7:10
20:28-29	3:10	9:6
20:34-35	4:2	9:7

10:8	3:4b-6	1:16
10:11	3:7	3:1-7
11:6	4:2	3:1
11:12	4:9	3:2
11:23	**Colossians**	3:7
11:28	1:6b	3:10
13:10	2:1	4:12
Galatians	3:8	5:8
2:6-8	3:21	6:20
2:11	3:23	**2 Timothy**
3:26-28	4:11	2:2
5:14	4:17	2:3
Ephesians	**1 Thessalonians**	2:4
1:11	1:2	2:23
2:20	1:6-7	4:2
3:10	2:11-12	4:6-7
4:1	2:14	4:16
4:12	4:11-12	**Titus**
4:16	5:11	1:5-9
4:29	5:12	1:5
5:15	**2 Thessalonians**	1:9
6:4	1:4	2:7-8
6:8	3:4	2:15
6:10-11	3:8	3:10
6:20	3:13	**Philemon**
Philippians	3:14-15	8
1:14	**1 Timothy**	11
2:3	1:5	15
2:20	1:12	21

CPSIA information can be obtained at www.ICGtesting.com
Printed in the USA
BVOW030034150812

297815BV00005B/3/P